The Bumper Book of

Crafty Activities

100+ creative ideas for kids

First published in Great Britain 2012

Search Press Limited
Wellwood, North Farm Road,
Tunbridge Wells, Kent TN2 3DR

Based on the following books published by Search Press:

Crafty Activities by Michelle Powell, Judy Balchin,
Clive Stevens and Tamsin Carter (2007) and

More Crafty Activities by Judy Balchin, Greta Speechley,
Michelle Powell, David Watson and Clive Stevens, (2008)

Text copyright © Michelle Powell, Judy Balchin,
Clive Stevens, Tamsin Carter, Greta Speechley and
David Watson, 2012

Photographs by Charlotte de la Bédoyère,
Search Press Studios
Photographs and design copyright © Search Press 2012

ISBN: 978-1-84448-793-6

Suppliers
If you have difficulty obtaining any of the materials and
equipment mentioned in this book, please visit the
Search Press website for details of suppliers:

www.searchpress.com

Acknowledgements
The Publishers would like to say a huge thank you
to all the children who appear in the photographs.
Finally, special thanks to Southborough Primary
School, Tunbridge Wells

When this sign is used in
the book it means that adult
supervision is needed.

REMEMBER!
Ask an adult to help you
when you see this sign.

Printed in China

The Bumper Book of
Crafty Activities

100+ creative ideas for kids

Search Press

Contents

Printing 5

Creative Lettering 31

Mosaics 57

Papier Mâché 83

Origami 109

Handmade Cards 135

Collage 161

Clay Modelling 187

Beadwork 213

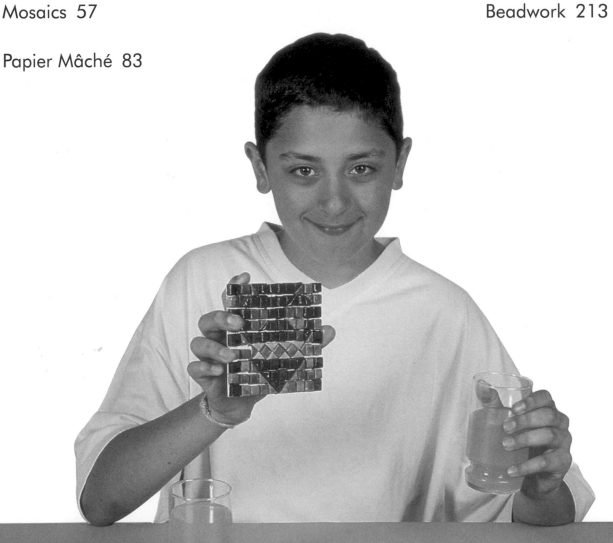

Decorative Painting 239

Papermaking 265

Paperfolding 291

About the authors 318

Printing

by Michelle Powell

Printing is a process that involves making marks and reproducing those marks again and again. The marks can be shapes, patterns, pictures or words. Even a footprint in the snow is a basic form of printing.

The need for printing grew out of the need for written communication. Over five-and-a-half thousand years ago, the first writing appeared in Egypt as groups of symbols in clay tablets. As writing developed it was used to record events and re-tell stories. The ancient Egyptians wrote in pictures called hieroglyphics – one picture would represent a whole word or just part of a word. The Greeks, Romans, Vikings and other civilizations all had their own way of writing.

In the ninth century AD, the Chinese developed a method of printing using a carved wooden seal. They used this print to stamp official documents. Later, they produced carved wooden blocks to represent characters. The carved eraser stamps used in the dominoes project on pages 18–19 are made in a similar way.

Traditional printing methods are still used today. In this section I have looked at a variety of different techniques for making prints. The beauty of printing rather than drawing or painting, is that you can reproduce the same image over and over again, using the same printing block, tool or stamp. In this way you can quickly create a very detailed design with lots of repetition, or you can print on many items. This makes printing the perfect technique if you want to make lots of greetings cards for your friends, print up items to decorate your bedroom, or make unusual gifts for your family.

The first projects in the section use natural and man-made objects for printing. When you start looking for things to print with, you will soon discover that hundreds of different items are suitable. Cotton reels, scouring pads, bubblewrap, corrugated card, pen lids, corks and leaves can all be used to create interesting patterns and shapes.

I have also included projects which show different ways of creating printing blocks. You can use polystyrene, erasers, potatoes, string, foam and even pipe cleaners to make a fantastic range of designs. There are patterns at the end of the section that you can work from, or you can use your own drawings and designs to create unique prints.

Printing enables you to decorate many different things, and with a little experience you will soon be creating printed masterpieces of your own.

The most important thing of all is to have fun when printing!

Natural Wrapping Paper and Gift Tag

You can use many natural objects to print with. Look around the garden for flat stones and pieces of bark or ask for a slice of your favourite fruit or vegetable. This project uses a real leaf.

When choosing your leaf look for a flat, fresh one. Turn it over and feel the back. Leaves that have veins that you can feel are the best for printing. There are so many different trees to choose from – oak, maple, beech and sycamore to name a few.

 Ink up the leaf using a rubber roller and a dye-based ink pad. Roll over the leaf a few times.

 Choose a leaf with an obvious vein pattern.

 Press the leaf firmly on to the paper. Smooth over it with your fingers.

 Repeat the leaf pattern all over the paper. Leave to dry.

8

5 Cut out a rectangle of thin card and fold it in half to make a gift tag. Use a hole punch to make a hole in the folded edge.

6 Print a leaf on the gift tag. Loop a piece of string through the hole and tie to secure.

FURTHER IDEAS
Try using your leaf design on envelopes, writing paper, cards and invitations.

Sea Monster Game

The inspiration for this fun fishing game comes from the classical sea monsters which feature in the tales of Ancient Greek mythology. You can use textured objects such as bubblewrap and cotton reels to print your own double-headed sea serpents and giant squid. You will need small, round magnets to make this game. These are available from craft shops.

I have used seven sea monsters for this game, but you can make any odd number. For details of how to play the game, turn to page 29.

For details of how to play the game, turn to page 29.

YOU WILL NEED

Textured objects, e.g. bubblewrap, cotton reels, scouring pads, sponges
Thin card • Scrap paper • Newspaper
Tracing paper • Carbon paper
Masking tape • Water-based paint
Sponge roller • Paintbrush
7 paperclips • 2 magnets
2 pencils • Scissors
String

1 Transfer a mythical sea monster shape on to a piece of thin card (see pages 28–29). Cut it out. Repeat until you have seven sea monsters in total.

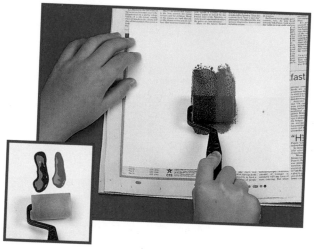

2 Place two stripes of different coloured paint on a piece of scrap paper. Run a sponge roller over both colours at once.

3 Choose a textured object such as bubblewrap, then use the roller to apply paint to one side of it. Turn the bubblewrap over then press it down on to the cut-out sea monster. Peel off to reveal the printed pattern. Leave to dry.

Continue, using different objects and colours, until all the sea monsters are decorated. Paint in the eyes then leave to dry. Repeat steps 2–4 on the back of all the sea monsters.

Attach a paperclip to the mouth of each sea monster.

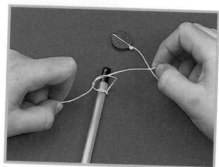

Tie a small magnet on to a piece of string. Tie the other end of the string on to a pencil. You are now ready to play the game.

FURTHER IDEAS
Tie your sea monsters to a coat hanger to create a colourful mobile.

Chinese Pencil Pot

If you are always losing your pencils and pens then this is the project for you. The pot is decorated with Chinese-style printed paper and gold trim is used to add the finishing touch.

A paint paste is spread thickly all over the paper then the design is created by scraping some of the paste away with a cardboard comb so that the paper shows through underneath. For best results use white paper and a darker coloured paint.

YOU WILL NEED
Cardboard tubing • Cardboard
Paper • Newspaper
Wallpaper paste • Washing-up liquid
Water-based paint • PVA glue
Small mixing bowl or dish
Paintbrush • Scissors
Length of trim

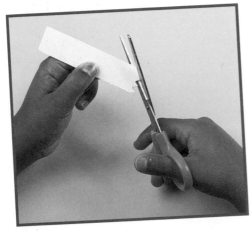

1 Use scissors to cut little V-shaped notches at one end of a small rectangle of cardboard to make a comb.

2 Mix up one cup of wallpaper paste with two teaspoons of paint and one teaspoon of washing-up liquid. Brush the paste mixture thickly on to your paper using a paintbrush.

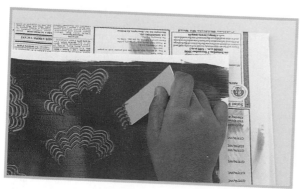

3 Use the cardboard comb to drag a pattern into the paste. Wipe the comb on some newspaper when it becomes clogged with paint.

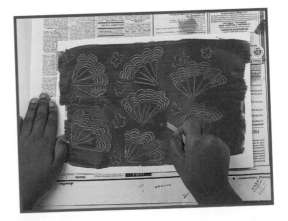

4 Use a small strip of cardboard to add details. Work quickly before the paste dries. When finished, leave to dry.

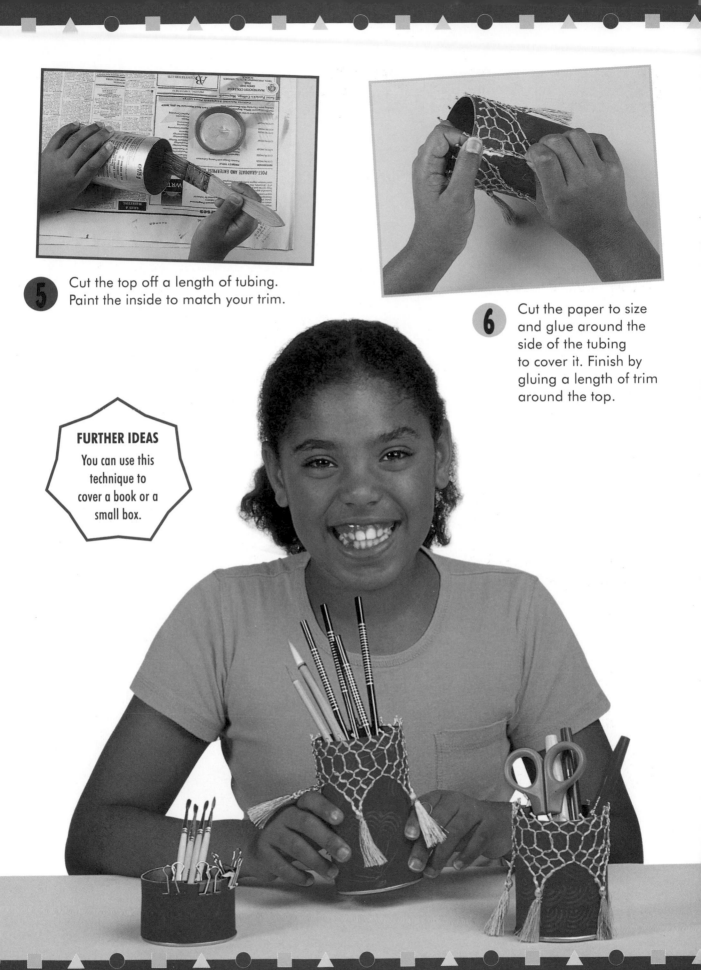

5 Cut the top off a length of tubing. Paint the inside to match your trim.

6 Cut the paper to size and glue around the side of the tubing to cover it. Finish by gluing a length of trim around the top.

FURTHER IDEAS

You can use this technique to cover a book or a small box.

Gecko T-shirt

The idea for this design comes from the paintings the Native American Indians used to decorate their tepees. I have chosen a gecko lizard for this T-shirt, but they painted many other designs. Some were used to encourage good spirits and fortunes. The paints they used were made from plants and soil, so the colours were natural and earthy.

This type of printing is called mono printing. Mono means 'one', and with this method of printing you can only make one print. This technique is ideal for transferring a colourful design on to fabric.

YOU WILL NEED

T-shirt • Acetate
Fabric paints • Paintbrush
Paper • Newspaper
Tracing paper • Carbon paper
Pencil • Masking tape
Iron • Ironing board

 Transfer the gecko design shown on page 29 on to paper (see page 28). Place a sheet of acetate over the design and tape it in place.

2 Paint over one section of the design using one colour of fabric paint.

3 Turn the acetate face down on to the front of your T-shirt. Rub over the back of the acetate with your hand.

4 Carefully peel off the acetate. Touch up the colour with a paintbrush if necessary.

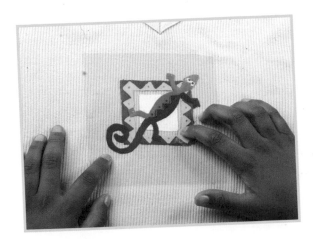

FURTHER IDEAS
Use glow-in-the-dark paint to create a unique T-shirt.

5 Repeat steps 1–4 with other colours to complete the design. Remember to line up the image carefully each time. When complete, leave the paint to dry thoroughly for twenty-four hours.

6 Turn the T-shirt inside out and place a piece of paper inside it. Iron over the design on the reverse side of the T-shirt. Ironing will fix the paints so that the colours do not come out when the T-shirt is washed.

! Make sure an adult helps you to iron the T-shirt.

Aztec Birthday Card

Bright, earthy colours and an Aztec sun design are used to create the Mexican theme for this original, hand-printed birthday card.

A piece of smooth, firm polystyrene (like that used for fast-food packaging) is used to create a printing block. This type of block can be used over and over again, so you can print lots of cards using the same design.

1 Cut out a small square of polystyrene.

2 Transfer the sun design shown on page 29 on to the polystyrene (see page 28). Use a blunt pencil to score over the design.

3 Press the front of the polystyrene square on to a rainbow ink pad.

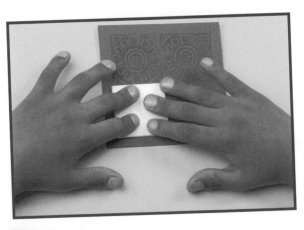

4 Press the polystyrene printing block into the corner of a piece of folded coloured card. Repeat in each corner.

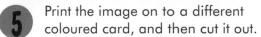
5 Print the image on to a different coloured card, and then cut it out.

6 Glue the design into the centre of the folded card.

FURTHER IDEAS
You can decorate an envelope to match your card.

Egyptian Dominoes

The Ancient Egyptians used pictures called hieroglyphics to tell stories. Hieroglyphic designs are used in this project to create picture dominoes as a variation on the traditional dominoes game. For details about how to play the game, turn to page 30.

You can create wonderfully detailed printing blocks by carving a design into an eraser using a lino cutter. An eraser is soft enough to cut into easily and it transfers the paint well when you start printing.

YOU WILL NEED

6 erasers • Lino cutter
Water-based paint • Paintbrush
Sponge • Coloured card
Newspaper • Tracing paper
Carbon paper
Pencil • Marker pen
Scissors • Ruler

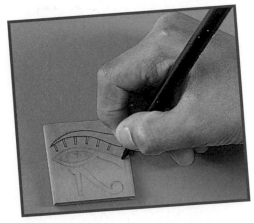

1 Transfer the six designs shown on page 30 on to six erasers (see page 28). Go over the outlines using a marker pen.

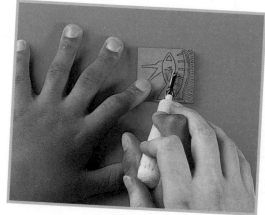

2 Use a lino cutter to carve out the areas around and within the designs. Cut with the blade pointing away, not towards you.

A lino cutter is sharp. Make sure you get an adult to help you when you use it.

3 Use a ruler and pencil to mark out twenty-one identical rectangles on coloured card large enough to print two images on. Cut them out using scissors.

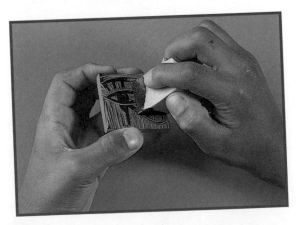

4 Use a sponge to apply paint to one of the designs on one of the erasers.

5

Press the eraser on to one end of one of the card rectangles. Repeat step 4 and continue printing. Make sure that each domino is different and that you have used each stamp six times.

Note The diagram on page 30 shows which pictures to put together to make a whole set of dominoes.

6

Add detailing to each of the designs using coloured paint and a paintbrush.

FURTHER IDEAS

Print one image on each piece of card. Make sure you have at least four of each design. Use these to play 'snap' with.

Modern Art Socks

You can get many great design ideas from looking at the work of modern artists. Try to recreate the colours and the patterns they have used. The designs in this project are inspired by the work of the French artist, Matisse.

Ordinary potatoes are used to print bold, lively images on to plain socks. Your potatoes will need to be quite fresh, so that they are still hard. Remember that the size of your design will be limited by the size of your potato.

YOU WILL NEED

Pair of plain socks
2 potatoes • Vegetable knife
Chopping board • Fabric paint
Paintbrush • Thin card
Newspaper • Pencil
Marker pen • Scissors
Iron • Ironing board

 Place the card template inside the sock.

1 Place one of your socks on a piece of thin card, then draw around it with a pencil. Cut out the shape.

! Vegetable knives are very sharp. Get an adult to help when you cut the potatoes.

3 Place two potatoes on a chopping board. Cut them in half using a vegetable knife.

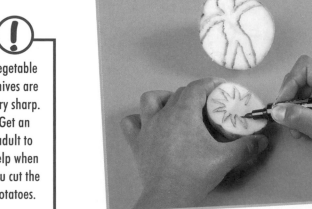

4 Use a marker pen to copy the designs shown on page 31 on to the potatoes.

Get an adult to help you cut out the designs.

5 Use a vegetable knife to cut down around the edge of the design, then across from the side of the potato.

6 Paint over the raised designs with fabric paint, then print them on to your sock. Repeat all the steps to decorate the other sock. Iron to fix the colours (see page 15).

FURTHER IDEAS
You can decorate lots of items using this technique — baseball hats, canvas shoes or T-shirts, for example.

Mosaic Chalk Board

Mosaic designs are normally made by cutting glass or coloured tiles into small pieces then cementing them on to a wall or floor to create a picture or pattern. The Ancient Greeks and Romans are famous for mosaics.

In this project, a piece of high-density foam is cut into small squares and stuck to a wooden block. The block is then used to print instant mosaic designs. You could use thick cardboard instead of wood, but this means that you cannot wash and re-use the block. Before you begin, measure your chalk board and decide what size the designs need to be before you trace them from page 29.

YOU WILL NEED
Chalk board
High-density foam
Square and rectangular wood off-cuts
or thick cardboard
Water-based paints • Paintbrush
Newspaper • Carbon paper
Tracing paper • Masking tape
Pencil • Scissors
PVA glue

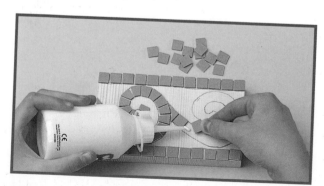

1 Transfer the designs shown on page 31 on to square and rectangular pieces of wood (see page 28).

2 Use scissors to cut a piece of high-density foam into small squares. Cut some of these squares into smaller, odd-shaped pieces.

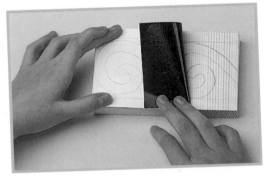

3 Glue the square foam pieces on to each piece of wood, following the lines of the designs. Fill in the gaps with the small odd-shaped pieces of foam.

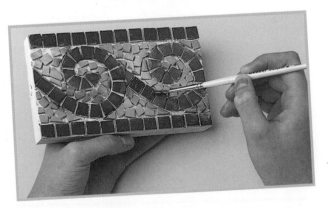

4 Paint over the raised foam images on both the square and rectangular printing blocks. Change colours where appropriate.

5 Press the square stamp on to one of the corners of the chalk board. Carefully lift the block off, apply more paint, then repeat at each corner.

6 Print the rectangular block around the edge of the chalk board to create a border. Re-apply paint between each print.

FURTHER IDEAS
You can use this technique to decorate the rim of an indoor plant pot.

Asian Cushion

This sumptuous cushion is printed with a design inspired by traditional Asian arts. The design is known as paisley and is often used to decorate the elaborate saris worn by Asian women. In India and surrounding countries, very bright colours are popular for clothes and decorations.

The printing block for this project is made out of string glued to a piece of thin card. For best results choose string that is smooth, thick and quite stiff, as this will hold its shape well.

YOU WILL NEED

Plain cushion
String • Thin card • Paper
Carbon paper • Tracing paper
Masking tape • Pencil • Scissors
Fabric paint • Sponge
Tea towel or piece of cloth
Iron and ironing board
PVA glue

 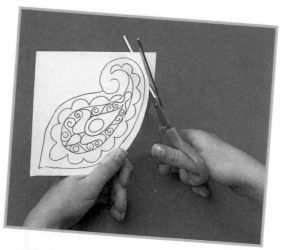

1 Transfer the paisley design shown on page 31 on to a piece of thin card. Cut it out, leaving a small border around the edge.

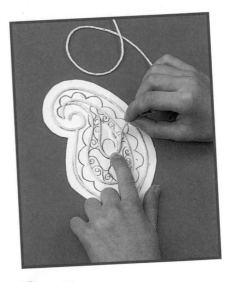

2 Glue string on to the card, following the line of the design.

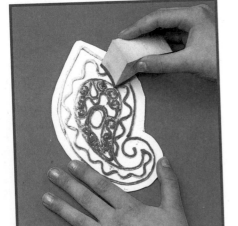

3 Apply fabric paint on to the string using a sponge.

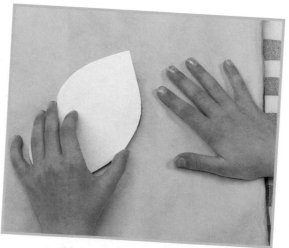

4 Place the cushion on a smooth and soft surface such as a folded tea towel. This will make it easier to print the design. Press the painted side of the string design on to the plain cushion.

5

Repeat steps 3–4 to cover the cushion, applying more paint to the string each time you make a print. Iron to fix the design (see page 15).

6 Place the cushion pad back inside the cover.

FURTHER IDEAS
You can use this technique to decorate a plain shoebag.

Primitive Clay Picture

The first recorded forms of art were the paintings on cave walls which were made by early settlers. The paintings usually showed images of men and animals and were painted in muted shades of red and brown. Like the Native Indians, early settlers used soil and clay to create a type of paint.

You can create your own cave paintings by printing with pipe cleaners into air-drying clay. The clay is soft, so you can push the pipe cleaner shapes into the clay to leave an impression. When the clay has dried, it can be painted with earthy colours.

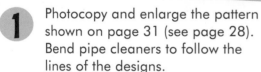

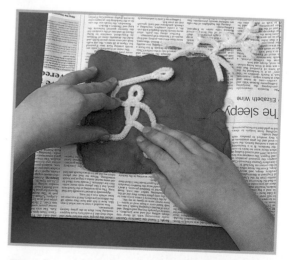

 Work small sections at a time, cutting the pipe cleaners as you go. Join the pieces together by twisting them.

 Photocopy and enlarge the pattern shown on page 31 (see page 28). Bend pipe cleaners to follow the lines of the designs.

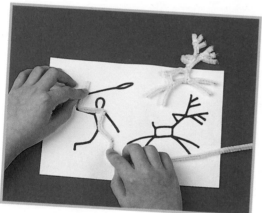

 Press a piece of clay with your fingers to flatten it into a square shape.

 Press the pipe cleaner designs into the clay to leave an impression. Remove them carefully then leave the clay to dry for twenty-four hours.

5 Sponge earthy-coloured paints randomly over the clay to create the effect of stone.

6 Use a paintbrush to paint around the shape of the designs so that they stand out.

FURTHER IDEAS
You can use this technique to make an unusual paperweight.

Patterns

You can trace the patterns on these pages straight from the book (follow steps 1–4). Alternatively, you can make them larger or smaller on a photocopier if you wish, and then follow steps 2–4.

Get an adult to help you photocopy the patterns.

Transferring a pattern on to another surface

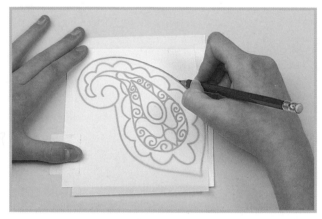

1 Place a piece of tracing paper over the pattern and then tape it down with small pieces of masking tape. Trace around the outline using a soft pencil.

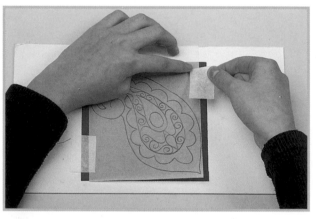

2 Place carbon paper on the surface you want to transfer the design on to. Place the tracing over the top and tape it in place.

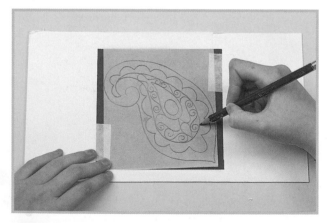

3 Trace over the outline with a pencil.

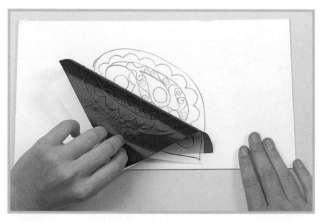

4 Remove the tracing paper and carbon paper to reveal the transferred image.

Patterns for the Sea Monster Game featured on pages 10–11.

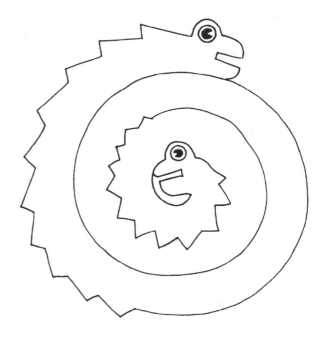

Pattern for the Gecko T-shirt featured on pages 14–15.

Pattern for the Aztec Birthday Card featured on pages 16–17.

1 1	1 2	1 3	1 4	1 5	1 6
2 2	2 3	2 4	2 5	2 6
3 3	3 4	3 5	3 6
4 4	4 5	4 6
5 5	5 6
6 6

The patterns shown below are for the Egyptian Dominoes featured on pages 18–19. They have all been given a number. Print your dominoes in the combinations shown here.

Rules for Dominoes

To play the game, deal each player seven dominoes face down. Leave the rest in a pile face down. Player 1 places a domino on the table; player 2 looks through their dominoes for a matching picture, and places that domino next to the first so that the pictures touch. Play continues in this way until a player cannot put a domino down. This player must pick up one of the spare dominoes and continue play. The winner is the first person to put down all of their dominoes. You can match two pictures at either end of the domino, and doubles can be played sideways.

1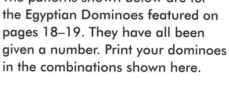

2

3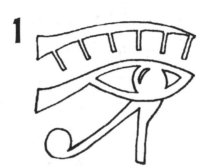

4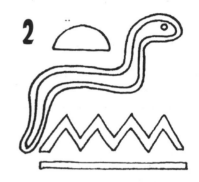

5

6

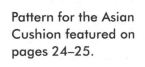
Pattern for the Asian Cushion featured on pages 24–25.

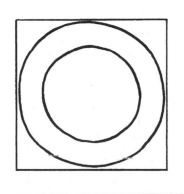

Patterns for the Mosaic Chalk Board featured on pages 22–23.

Patterns for the Modern Art Socks featured on pages 20–21. These cannot be transferred on to a potato using the technique shown on page 26, so you will need to copy them carefully yourself. Adjust the sizes according to the sizes of your potatoes.

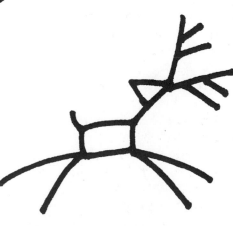

Patterns for the Primitive Clay Picture featured on pages 26–27.

Creative Lettering by Judy Balchin

Imagine a world with no letters – no books, signs or labels, no way to leave a message for your parents or to write to friends. Well, that is how it was a long time ago. There were no letters; they actually had to be invented.

Many years ago the American Indians used pictures called pictograms as a memory guide to remind them of events and songs when telling stories. As time went on and more complicated information needed to be exchanged or remembered, symbols were created to represent ideas or things. We can still see this today in the Chinese alphabet. Every idea or thing has its own symbol and believe it or not, a Chinese scholar must know over fifteen thousand symbols to write his books. The ancient Egyptians used another complicated system called hieroglyphics. We all know our ABC, but did you know that the letter A was once a hieroglyphic symbol of an eagle and B was a crane?

Over time, alphabets had to change and become simpler. The first simple alphabet was invented in Assyria in the fourteenth century BC. It was called cuneiform and was made up of lines and wedge shapes. It had thirty letters and was used by merchants to record their business dealings. The twenty-six letters we use today are derived from the Greek alphabet. In fact the word 'alphabet' is made from the first two letters of the Greek alphabet, alpha and beta.

We are surrounded by letters. Advertisers are extremely competitive and creative with their lettering styles as they entice you to buy their product. Perhaps you could try having a 'letter awareness' day. Get up in the morning, brush your teeth and look at the lettering on your toothpaste tube. Read the cereal packet over breakfast and see what letters are used. Look at book covers at school and while you eat your lunch, study the food wrappers. Television too offers us a variety of letter styles. It is amazing just how creative you can be with letters.

Now that you know the wonderful history of the alphabet and just how important lettering is to our everyday lives, we can have some fun. By the time you have worked your way through this section you will be able to tell the difference between 'serif' and 'sans serif' letters. You will notice 'drop shadows' on letters and begin to understand how important colour is. With a few pens and some paper you will be able to create your own letters and make cards, invitations, writing paper, bookmarks, posters and much more. I hope that this section inspires you to continue with this fascinating hobby.

Techniques

Take time to read through this techniques section before you start the projects. The alphabets and patterns that you will need are on pages 52–56. You can transfer them on to your paper with transfer paper.

Ask an adult to help you enlarge the letters and patterns on a photocopier.

Transferring letters and patterns

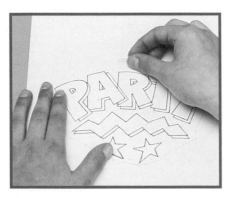

 Enlarge the pattern on a photocopier and cut it out. Lay it on a sheet of paper and tape the top with a piece of masking tape.

 Slip the transfer paper face-down under the pattern and tape it at the bottom to keep it in place.

3 Trace around the outline of the pattern with a pencil to transfer the design on to the paper.

4 Remove the transfer paper, then go over the outline with a black pen. Leave to dry for five minutes.

 Rub out any lines or smudges with an eraser and fill in the design with coloured pens.

Note Remember to put the tops back on your pens.

Copying letters

You will be asked to copy letters from the alphabets at the back of this section. Planning your lettering is important. Always work in pencil before going over the letters with a pen.

 Lightly draw in the guidelines for the lettering. A guideline is the line on which your letters sit. It may be straight, curved or wavy.

Note Cut a star shape around the design, or choose your own shape.

2 Pencil in the letters using the alphabet as a guide (see page 52). This dot serif alphabet is the easiest one to start with as it is based on neat writing.

3 Go over the pencilled letters with a coloured pen, adding dots to the ends and joints of the letters. When the pen has dried, remove any visible pencil lines with an eraser.

Rocket Birthday Card

Make your own dazzling range of cards using coloured pens and paper. The 'dot serif' alphabet used here is the easiest alphabet to create. All you have to do is print your message clearly, then add dots to the ends and joints of the letters. You can bring a sense of movement into the words by slanting the letters in different ways. A pattern has been provided (see page 57), but you might like to try this project without using the pattern. Practise on scrap paper first.

1 Transfer the pattern from page 57 on to white paper (see page 34).

2 Go over the outlines with a black felt-tipped pen. Leave to dry then rub out all the pencil lines.

3 Run a coloured line around the black lettering.

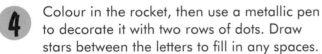

4 Colour in the rocket, then use a metallic pen to decorate it with two rows of dots. Draw stars between the letters to fill in any spaces.

5 Cut out the design.

6 Fold a sheet of metallic card in half and glue your design in place.

FURTHER IDEAS
You can create lots of cards for other occasions. Decorate them with colourful shapes and images.

Balloon Party Invitation

Send a special party invitation to your friends. A 'sans serif' alphabet with a 'drop shadow' is used for the lettering. Serifs are the lines that extend across the ends of the letters and 'Sans serif' means without serifs. Compare the alphabets on pages 54 and 55 to see the difference between 'serif' and 'sans serif' letters. A 'drop shadow' is a thick line which is usually drawn down one side and along the bottom of a letter, which makes it really stand out. This type of lettering is often used on food and sweet wrappers as it is bold and eye-catching.

YOU WILL NEED
Coloured card
Coloured felt-tipped pens
Black felt-tipped pen
Curling ribbon • Transfer paper
Masking tape • Pencil
Scissors • Eraser

1 Transfer the basic pattern from page 57 on to coloured card (see page 34). Go over the outline of the letters and designs with a black felt-tipped pen. Fill in the drop shadow.

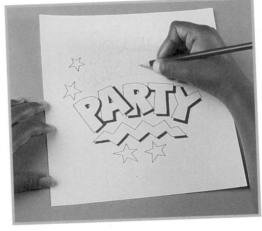

2 Draw two curved lines on the top half of the balloon. Lightly pencil in 'you are invited to a' using the alphabet on page 52 as a guide.

3 Outline the lettering with a brightly coloured pen. Leave to dry for a few minutes, then rub out any visible pencil lines.

Fill in the word 'party' and the zig-zag shape underneath with the same colour. Fill in the stars using a different colour, then add some curly lines.

5 Cut out the invitation. Tie a piece of paper ribbon around the knot of the balloon.

6 Lightly pencil in some guidelines on the back of the invitation, then write down your message.

FURTHER IDEAS

Write your name in the balloon and fill in the letters with lots of different colours.

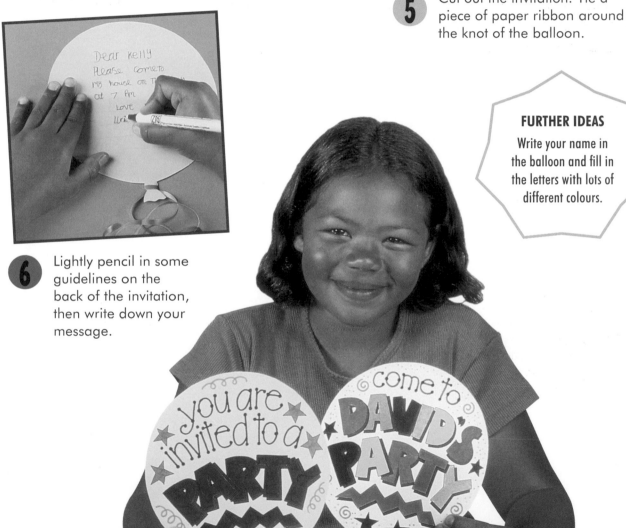

Alien Door Plaque

A design can look fun if you combine an illustration with the lettering and then decorate each letter with different colours and patterns. The door plaque uses the 'line serif' alphabet on page 55, where lines are drawn across the ends of the letters, so that they extend slightly beyond the letter. Can you spot 'serif' letters in your books?

 Transfer the pattern shown on page 57 on to white card (see page 34), then go over the outline with a black felt-tipped pen. Leave to dry.

 Fill in each of the letters with a different design. Use lots of colours.

 Use the dot serif alphabet on page 52 to pencil in 'my room' underneath and then outline with a coloured pen. Leave to dry and rub out all the pencil lines.

 Colour in the alien.

5 Draw a coloured border around the panel.

6 Cut out the plaque, leaving a small border around the edge.

FURTHER IDEAS
Use another alphabet and different colours to personalise a journal, school book or notebook.

! Ask an adult to help you attach the plaque to your door. You can use low-tack masking tape or removable adhesive.

Illuminated Bookmark

The inspiration for this project is taken from beautifully illuminated old manuscripts. These were created by monks using quill pens and paints, and the first capital letter on a page was always decorated with gold leaf and bright colours. Water-based paint and a metallic marker pen are used to create an illuminated bookmark. Use a dark colour for your own initial so that the metallic pen work really stands out.

YOU WILL NEED

Dark coloured card
Light coloured paper
Metallic marker pen
Water-based paint • Small paintbrush
Transfer paper • Masking Tape
Pencil • Eraser • Ruler
Scissors • PVA glue
Hole punch • Ribbon

1 Transfer a letter from the alphabet on page 53 on to light coloured paper (see page 34). Paint it using a dark colour. Leave to dry.

2 Use the alphabet pattern as a guide. Outline the letter and swirls with a metallic marker pen. Draw the inner lines. Leave to dry.

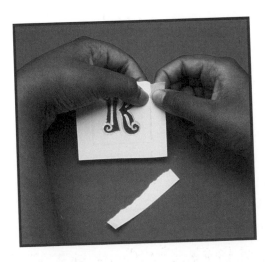

3 With a ruler and pencil, draw a square around the letter. Cut around the square leaving a small border, then tear the edges following the lines.

4 Draw a rectangle on dark card and tear the edges. Colour the edges of the square and the rectangle with a metallic marker pen.

5 Punch a hole at the top of the rectangle with a hole punch and glue the letter below it. Add swirls around the square with the metallic pen, then transfer the pattern shown on page 57 on to the area below the letter (see page 34).

6 Thread the bookmark with matching ribbon. Fold the ribbon in half, push the loop through the hole and pull the ends through the loop.

FURTHER IDEAS
By changing the initial and the colours you can make bookmarks for all your friends.

Personalised Paper

Creating your own personalised writing paper will give your letters a distinctive look. The letters are drawn in boxes which are cut out, arranged on a sheet of paper, then glued into place. The design can be photocopied many times and each copy can then be decorated with colours and motifs of your choice.

YOU WILL NEED
White paper
Black felt-tipped pen
Coloured felt-tipped pens
Ruler • Pencil
Scissors • PVA glue

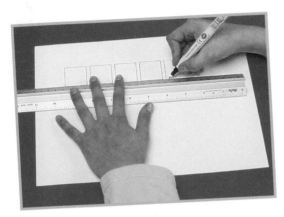

1 Count the letters in your first name. Draw the same number of 3cm (1¼in) squares on a piece of paper and outline them with a black felt-tipped pen.

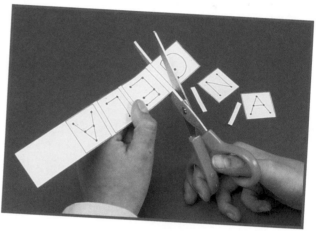

2 Choose an alphabet from the back of the book (see pages 52–56). Use a pencil to copy each letter of your name on to a square. Go over the outline of the letters with a black felt-tipped pen. Leave to dry, rub out any visible pencil lines, then cut out the squares.

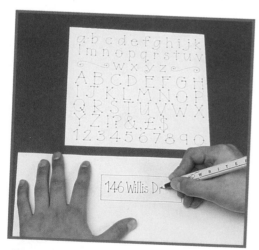

3 Draw a rectangle 3cm x 9cm (1¼in x 3¾in) and outline it in black. Write your address within it and then cut out the rectangle.

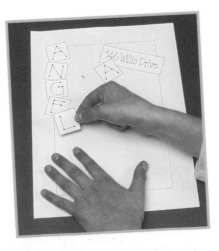

4 Use a ruler to draw a border line 3cm (1¼in) from the edges of a sheet of white paper. Glue the squares down the left-hand edge of the border, then glue the rectangle in the bottom right-hand corner.

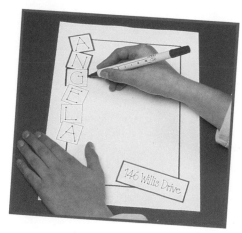

 Cover the outer border with a swirling pattern using a pale colour, then decorate it with darker spirals.

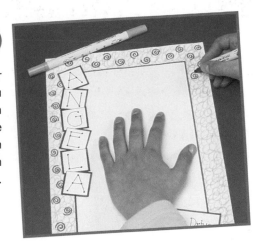

 Photocopy your letterhead as many times as you wish. Edge the border, the address panel and each square with a coloured pen.

!

Ask an adult to help you photocopy the letterhead.

FURTHER IDEAS

Choose a different alphabet and photocopy your design on to coloured paper. Decorate the border with squares, triangles or circles.

Snow White Poster

Large letters and bright colours are needed for a title when you are making a poster. This makes it more eye-catching. It is easier to cut the letters out of paper and to arrange them on a card base along with an information panel. When you are satisfied with the design, glue all the letters down.

YOU WILL NEED
Coloured and white paper
Sparkly card
Coloured card
Tracing paper • Pencil
Coloured felt-tipped pens
Scissors • PVA glue

!
Ask an adult to help you enlarge the letters on a photocopier.

 Trace the letters for the title using the alphabet on page 56. Enlarge the letters on a photocopier so that the longest word fits comfortably across a sheet of paper. Cut the letters out.

 Lay the letters on the sparkly card and draw around them.

3 Cut the letters out and arrange them across the top of the coloured card. Glue them in position. Cut and glue a rectangle of sparkly card to fit within the bottom half of the card.

Cut out a piece of white paper slightly smaller than the rectangle of sparkly card. Using the letters on page 52 as a guide, pencil your message on to the white rectangle. Go over the words with coloured pens.

Glue the panel on to the sparkly card.

Cut out stars from coloured paper and glue them around the edge of your poster.

FURTHER IDEAS
Make more posters to broadcast special messages or school news. Illustrate them with different shapes and patterns.

Hobby Box

The style and decoration of lettering tells us quite a lot. This container needs a bold, brightly coloured label which shouts 'paints'. The letters have a drop shadow and are overlapped slightly to give them a three dimensional look. The colours of the box and label complement each other, which creates a bright, stylish look.

YOU WILL NEED

Round cardboard box 16cm diameter x 10cm high (6¼in x 4in)
White paper • Pencil
Black felt-tipped pen
Coloured felt-tipped pens • Scissors
Acrylic paints
Small and large paintbrushes
PVA glue

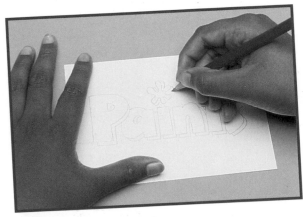

1 Draw the guidelines on white paper with a pencil. Copy the word 'Paints' using the alphabet on page 54 as a guide. Replace the dot over the 'i' with a splash shape, then add a drop shadow to the splash.

2 Use a black felt-tipped pen to go over the outlines of the letters, then fill in the drop shadow. Run wavy lines along the top of the letters to look like dripping paint.

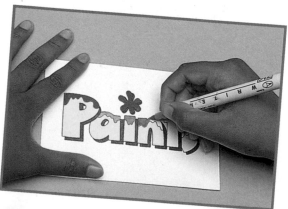

3 Fill in the letters with a bright colour, then fill in the splash and drips with different colours.

4 Cut around the letters, leaving a 0.5cm (¼in) border of white paper.

5 Use acrylic paints and a large paintbrush to paint the box and lid with bright colours. Draw splash shapes over the lid with a black felt-tipped pen. Leave to dry, then paint them in with bright colours using a small paintbrush.

6 Glue the finished label to the front of the box.

FURTHER IDEAS
Make a jewellery box using pastel colours and sparkly letters, or a treasure box using metallic colours.

School Project Folder

By now you will be getting more confident with your lettering. This project is great fun and you can really be creative! Each letter is transformed into an illustration. The first letter is 'P' – and P is for pencil, so you could draw a pencil in the shape of the letter P. The next letter is 'R' and R is for ribbon. Try to think of different things for each letter in the word 'Project'.

YOU WILL NEED
Coloured folder
Pencil • Ruler
White paper
Black felt-tipped pen
Coloured felt-tipped pens
PVA glue

Spend a little time planning what you want the letters to be. Write them down on a piece of paper and alongside each one make a list of things beginning with that letter. Try drawing a few of them to see how they will look.

2 Use a pencil and ruler to draw seven 6cm (2¼in) squares on a piece of white paper. Leave a gap of about 3cm (1¼in) between the squares.

3 Use a pencil and draw one illustrated letter on each square.

4 Go over the outlines of each letter with a black felt-tipped pen, then fill them in with different colours.

5

Cut around each box, leaving a small border. Now tear the edges of the squares following the lines.

6

Place the torn squares on a scrap piece of paper. Add a coloured border around the edges of each square.

7

Arrange the squares on your folder, then glue them into place.

FURTHER IDEAS

Create an alphabet using a different animal for each letter, or decorate your folder with fantasy figures.

Alphabets

These alphabets can be copied or traced on to tracing paper, then transferred on to your writing surface with transfer paper. They can also be enlarged on a photocopier if you are making a poster.

If you want to photocopy these letters, ask an adult to help you.

Dot serif

Illuminated

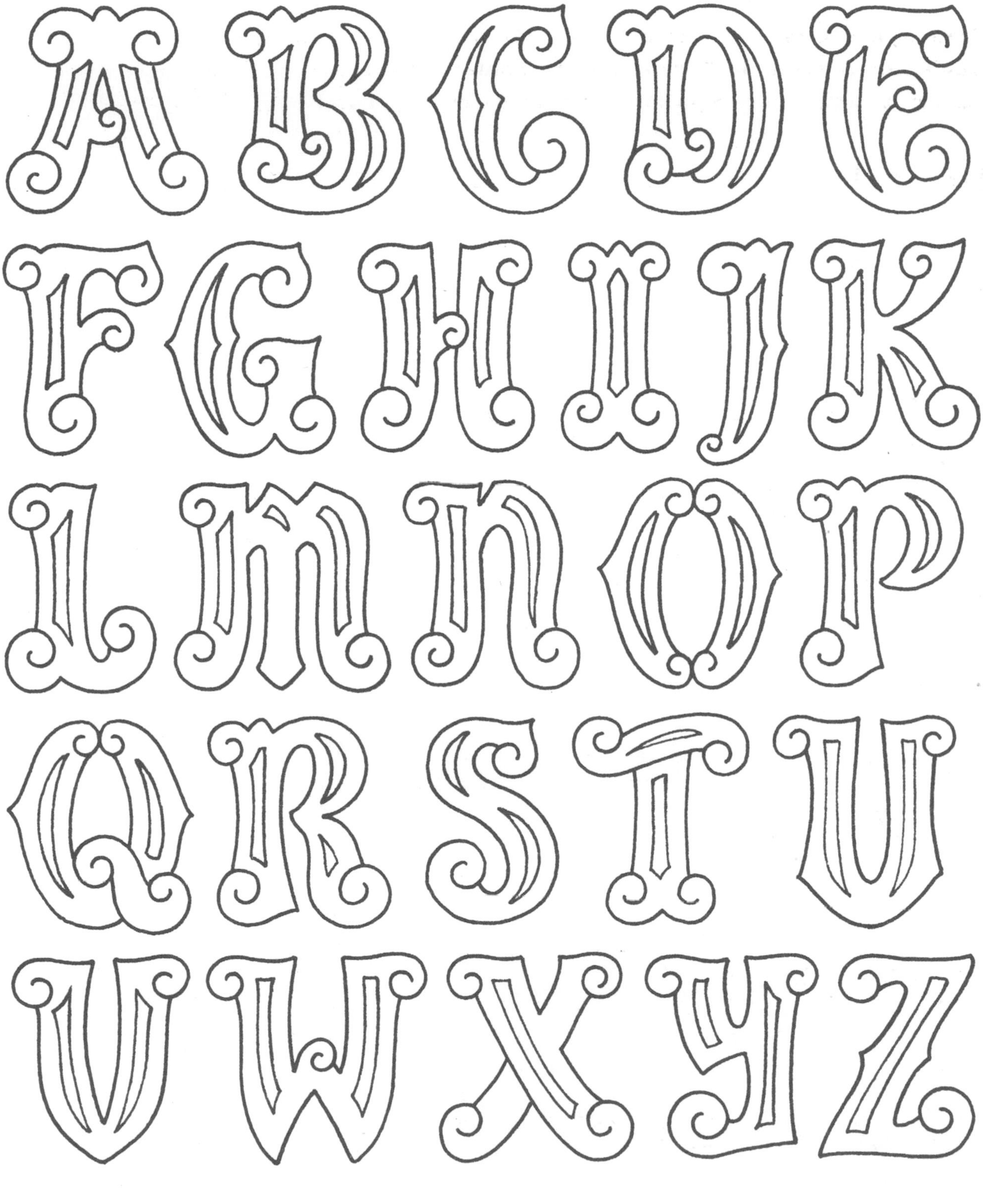

Block sans serif with drop shadow

Line serif

abcdefghij
klmnopqrs
tuvwxyz
ABCDEFG
HIJKLMN
OPQRSTUV
WXYZ!?&£$
1234567890

Rounded sans serif

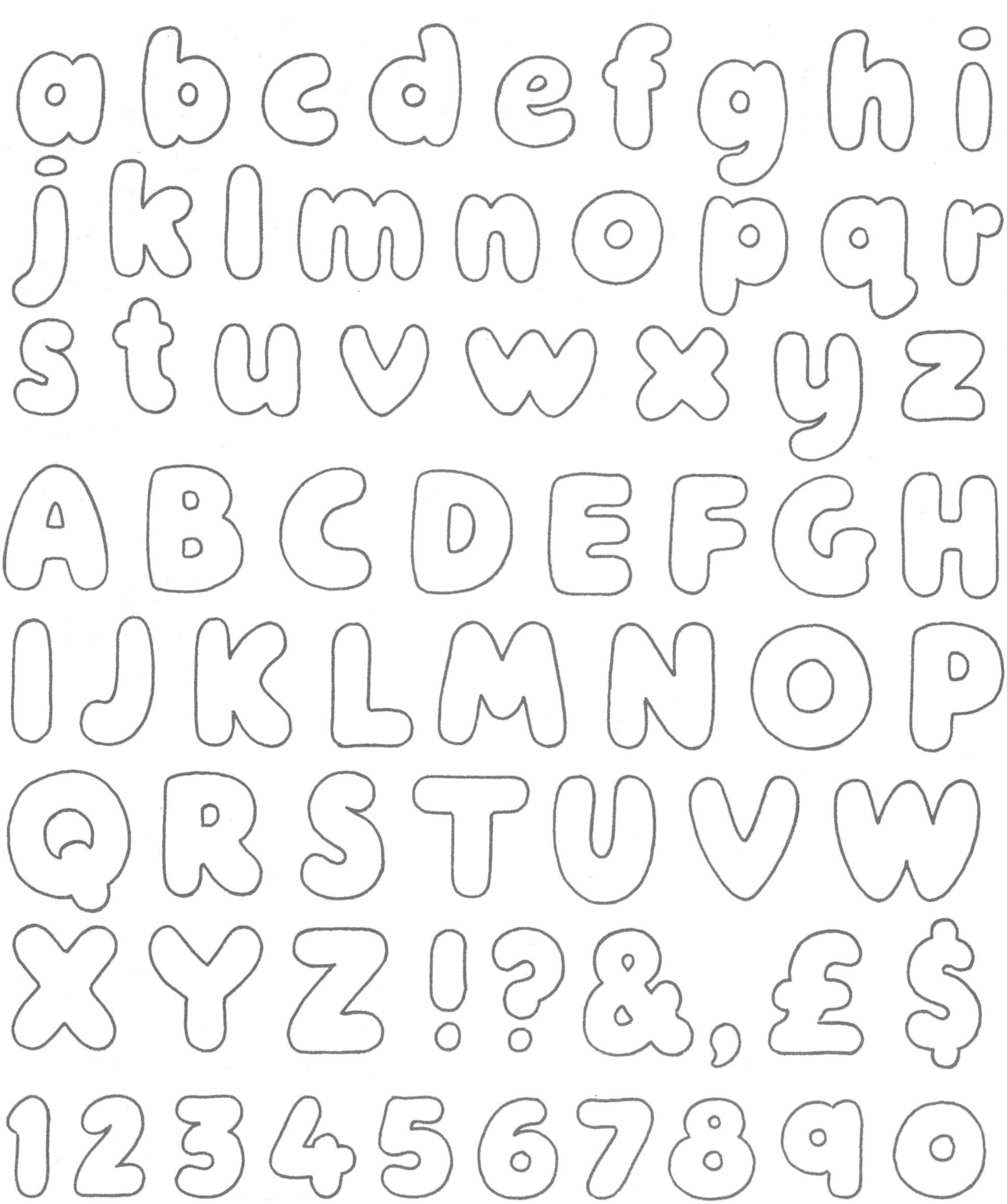

a b c d e f g h i
j k l m n o p q r
s t u v w x y z

A B C D E F G H
I J K L M N O P
Q R S T U V W
X Y Z ! ? & , £ $
1 2 3 4 5 6 7 8 9 0

Patterns

Ask an adult to help you enlarge the patterns on a photocopier.

Pattern for the Alien Door Plaque featured on pages 40–41.

Pattern for the Illuminated Bookmark featured on pages 42–43.

Pattern for the Balloon Party Invitation featured on pages 38–39.

Pattern for the Rocket Birthday Card featured on pages 36–37.

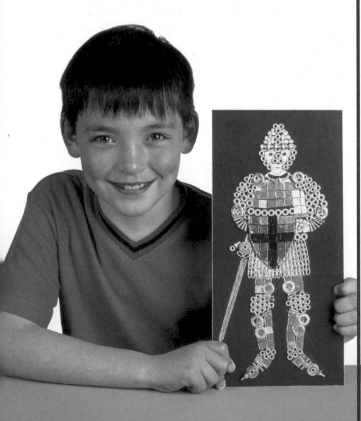

Mosaics

by Michelle Powell

Traditional mosaics are beautiful works of art. They are created with many small pieces of clay, glass, stone and other hard materials, which are set closely together on a firm surface to create a decorative design or picture.

The earliest mosaics date back to 3000 BC when they were usually created as a type of floor decoration made of small coloured pebbles. Later, glass, marble and clay were coloured then cut into small cubes or tiles. These were used to decorate the floors, walls and ceilings inside important buildings. A thick layer of plaster would be applied to the wall, then a picture or design was painted on to the surface while it was still wet. Before the plaster dried, matching coloured cubes or tiles were pushed into the surface to create the mosaic.

Large mosaics took a long time to make and were expensive, so they were very precious and a sign of great wealth. They were mostly used to decorate the inside of churches and religious buildings. Early Christian mosaics show figures and animals with decorative borders. In Islam, temples were decorated with beautiful designs of leaves and palm trees with a vibrant gold background. The Greeks often decorated their floors with dark and light pebble mosaics.

The ancient Egyptians made mosaic jewellery for their kings by setting tiny pieces of turquoise, precious stones and enamel into gold. On page 68 you will see how you can create a similar type of jewellery using pasta painted gold and turquoise. Gold and turquoise were also used to decorate statues and pottery items made by the ancient craft workers of Latin America. The Greeks and Romans made huge mosaics from handmade coloured clay tiles and our coaster project on page 72 shows you how to make your own clay mosaic tiles.

Some early mosaics can still be seen today, as they have not worn away over time. Now, small coloured glass squares and highly glazed clay tiles are especially made, and although they take a long time to create and are very expensive, mosaics are still being made by skilled crafts people.

Insect Greetings Card

It is very easy to make attractive mosaic greetings cards for your family and friends using your own drawings or paintings. Make sure you paint or draw them on thick card using brightly coloured, bold designs. Strong images and patterns work best, as fine detail will be lost when the picture is cut into mosaic pieces. Draw a grid on to the front of the picture or photograph (see step 4) and cut along the lines to create your mosaic pieces.

YOU WILL NEED

Thin card
Medium weight card
Carbon paper • Tracing paper
Masking tape • Pencil
Scissors • Ruler
Water-based paints or coloured pens
Paintbrush • Glue stick
Cocktail stick

1 Fold a piece of thin card in half and place it to one side.

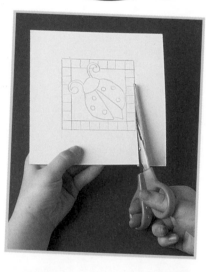

2 Transfer the insect pattern shown on page 81 on to a piece of medium weight card. Cut around the edge.

3 Use coloured paints or pens to fill in the design.

4 Use a pencil and ruler to join up the lines on the border – to form a grid on the front of the design.

 5

Cut along each line using scissors. Carefully lay the pieces down in order as they are cut out.

6

Carefully glue the pieces in the right order on to the front of the folded card. Leave a 2mm ($\frac{1}{12}$in) gap between each piece, using a cocktail stick as a guide.

FURTHER IDEAS

Use a colour photocopy of a favourite photograph instead of drawing your own picture.

African Mask

Masks were worn in African tribal war dances to make the wearer look more ferocious. The dancers would also use body adornments and sometimes special clothing, which added to the drama and atmosphere of the dance. You can make your own African mosaic mask using small squares and triangles of thin coloured high-density foam, felt or thin card. These soft materials are excellent for masks as they are more comfortable than some of the harder materials that are available.

YOU WILL NEED
Coloured high-density foam
Carbon paper • Tracing paper
Masking tape • Pencil
Scissors • Felt tipped pen
PVA glue • Hole punch
Shearing elastic

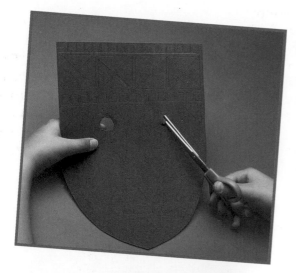

1 Transfer the mask pattern shown on page 81 on to a piece of high-density foam. Cut around the basic shape. Hold the mask up to your face, then carefully feel around on the front for the position of your eyes. Ask a friend to mark in their position with a felt-tipped pen, then cut out the eye holes using scissors.

2 Use the pattern as a rough guide. Choosing different colours, cut squares, triangles and wedge shapes from high-density foam.

3 Glue the pieces on to the mask using PVA glue.

 4

Cut out the nose from another piece of high-density foam and glue it into position. Cut out two circles for the nostrils and glue them on to the nose. Leave the glue to dry for half an hour.

 5 Use a hole punch to make a hole on either side of the mask, approximately 1cm (½in) in from the edge.

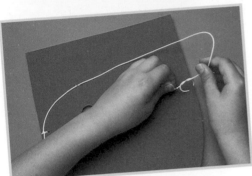

 6

Cut a piece of shearing elastic so that it is long enough to fit around your head. Tie each end through the holes in the mask.

FURTHER IDEAS

Choose an animal and make a fun mask, or choose different colours and create your own African mask.

Knight in Armour Picture

In the Middle Ages battling knights wore armour made of metal sheets and chain mail, which protected them from injury. In order to make this knight look more realistic, metal nuts, bolts, screws, washers and chain have been used, along with coloured and silver foils. You do not have to use any of these – just create the knight with whatever you have. Real chain has been used to create the chain mail. You can buy this from most **DIY** and home improvement stores.

 1

Transfer the knight in armour and shield patterns shown on page 81 on to a piece of thick card. Paint in the knight's face using a small paintbrush.

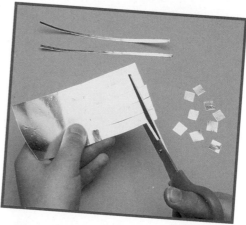

 2

Cut silver foil into small squares, triangles and wedge shapes for the armour. Cut out two strips long enough for the sword.

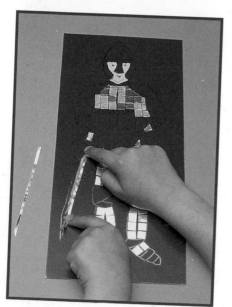

 3

Glue the foil on to the knight using PVA glue.

 4

Roll pieces of silver foil into small balls. Use PVA glue to attach them to the cuff on the armour, and the helmet.

5

Position the nuts, bolts, washers, screws and chain carefully on the knight. Glue in place with PVA glue.

!

If you decide to include chain, ask an adult to pull it apart with pliers, to make the correct lengths.

6

Cut out squares of coloured foil. Decorate the shield with the squares and washers then glue them into position with PVA glue. Leave to dry overnight.

FURTHER IDEAS

Make a metal robot picture using the same techniques, or create a shiny alien.

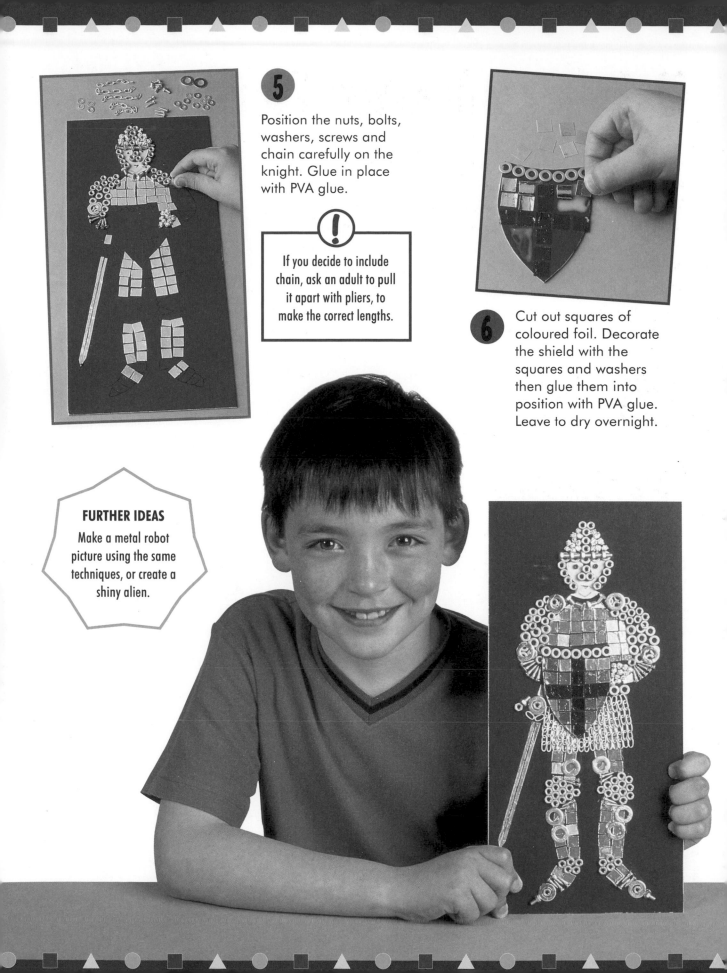

Indian Elephant Shoebag

In India, elephants are often seen at festivals wearing bright, colourful decorative saddlecloths and elaborate headdresses. Using coloured felt or fabrics, feathers and pretty gold or metallic coloured trims, you can create a fabric Indian elephant mosaic on a plain shoe or toiletries bag. If you do not have one that is suitable, ask an adult to make a simple bag out of a rectangle of fabric. Fold this in half, sew the bottom edges together, then the side edges. Turn the top edge over to the inside to form a hem, then sew along the bottom edge, leaving a gap at the side seam. Thread the cord through the hem and tie a knot at the end.

YOU WILL NEED
Fabric shoebag
Grey and coloured felt
Carbon paper • Tracing paper
Masking tape • Pencil
2 small feathers • Sequins
Metallic coloured trim
Scissors • PVA glue

 Cut grey felt into small squares and wedge shapes.

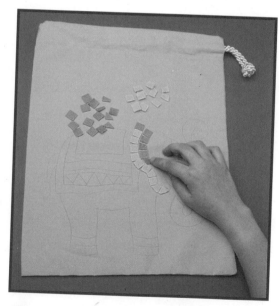

 Transfer the elephant design shown on page 82 on to your shoebag. Stick the grey felt squares and wedge shapes on to the elephant using PVA glue.

 Use different colours and cut some more felt into small squares and wedge shapes. Glue them in position.

Use PVA glue to attach small feathers to the headdress, and use sequins to decorate the saddlecloth.

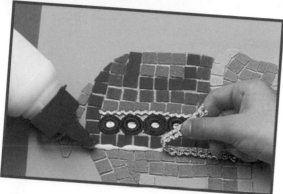

5 Glue metallic coloured trim around the headdress and the base of the saddlecloth.

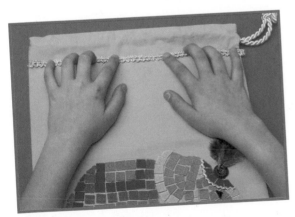

6 Glue metallic coloured trim around the top of the bag to decorate it. Leave to dry overnight.

Note The design on this shoebag is only glued on and therefore the bag should not be washed. If it gets dirty, carefully sponge it clean.

FURTHER IDEAS
Decorate a pencil case, school bag, baseball hat, T-shirt or jacket. Change the colours for different effects.

Egyptian Eagle Necklace

YOU WILL NEED

Small pasta shells and tubes
Thick card • Carbon paper
Tracing paper • Masking tape • Pencil
Metallic and coloured water-based paint
Paintbrush • Newspaper
3 lengths of shearing elastic 80cm
(31½in) long
Scissors • PVA glue
Hole punch

Beautiful gold and precious stone jewellery has been found in the tombs of ancient Egyptian pharaohs. You can make your own dazzling Egyptian mosaic jewellery using dried pasta – all sorts of different shapes are available. Look out for small shells and tubes that can be threaded like beads on to shearing elastic. The pasta is painted using coloured and metallic water-based paints in the same colours as the gold and precious stones used in Egyptian jewellery.

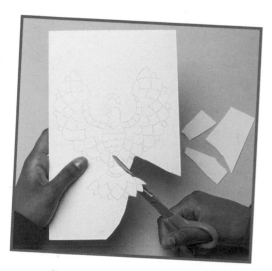

 Transfer the eagle pattern shown on page 82 on to thick card. Carefully cut it out.

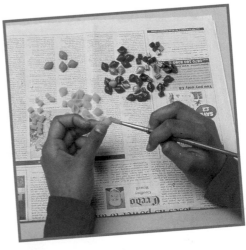

 Cover your work surface with newspaper. Paint the pasta shells and tubes with metallic and coloured paint. Leave the pieces to dry and wash your hands thoroughly.

Note Do not cook or eat the pasta after it has been painted.

 Use a hole punch to make three holes at the edge of the eagle's wings.

5 Tie three lengths of shearing elastic through the holes on one side of one wing. Thread pasta tubes on to the elastic.

Note String can be used instead of elastic.

4 Glue the pasta shells and tubes in place using PVA glue.

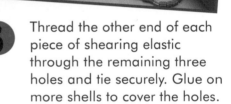

6 Thread the other end of each piece of shearing elastic through the remaining three holes and tie securely. Glue on more shells to cover the holes.

FURTHER IDEAS

Create a scarab beetle bracelet to match your necklace using the same techniques. Or look for other Egyptian designs and make your own jewellery using different colours.

Maths Biscuits

Mosaics can even be created using edible items like the small coloured sweets in this project. Here, candy coated chocolate sweets are attached to plain biscuits using icing. The quantities given make enough icing for four large biscuits. If you want to decorate more, you will need to make more icing. Use everyday kitchen utensils to make the icing and not things that you would normally use for painting, and remember to wash your hands well before you start to decorate the biscuits.

 Place six heaped dessertspoons of icing sugar into a bowl.

2 Add four teaspoons of lemon juice.

3 Stir the icing and lemon juice together until all the lumps are gone.

Note The icing should be like a stiff paste. If it is too runny, add more icing sugar. If it is too dry, add a drop more lemon juice.

4 Spoon a small quantity of icing over a biscuit and use the back of a teaspoon to spread it out.

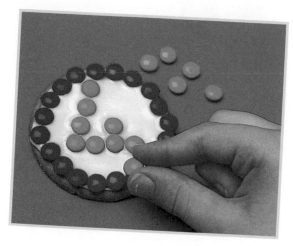

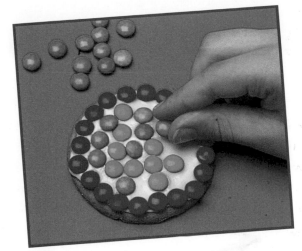

5 Press coloured sweets into the wet icing around the edge of the biscuit. Use a different colour to create a number in the middle.

6 Fill in the spaces around the number with another colour. Leave the biscuit until the icing is set.

FURTHER IDEAS
Why not mosaic your name on top of your birthday cake, or decorate some biscuits with simple shapes.

Grecian Coaster

The Greeks and Romans used small clay tiles to make their mosaics. In this project mosaic tiles are made using air-drying clay. The rolled out clay is soft enough to cut with a knife and most of the pieces are either squares or triangles, so the design can only have straight edges. When the clay is dry, it is painted with traditional Greek colours and the coaster is then sealed with PVA glue to protect it.

YOU WILL NEED
Air-drying clay • Thick card
Newspaper • Knife
Wooden rolling pin • Ruler
Water-based paint
Large and small paintbrushes
Scissors • PVA glue

1 Cover your work surface with newspaper. Take a ball of clay, roughly the size of a tennis ball, and roll it out to a thickness of between 0.5cm and 0.8cm (¼in and ⅜in).

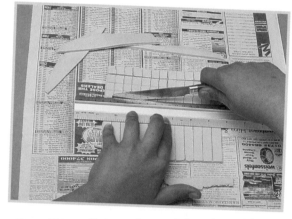

2 Trim off the edges of the clay with a knife, using a ruler as a guide. Cut vertical lines approximately 1cm (½in) apart. Cut horizontal lines in the same way to form small clay squares.

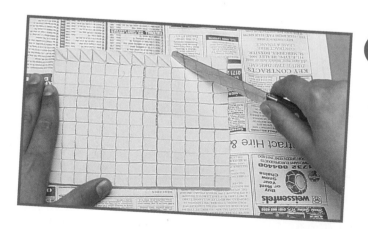

3 Cut a few of the squares diagonally to make triangles. Leave the clay to dry for two days.

Knives can be sharp. Ask an adult to help you cut the clay.

Use a small paintbrush and different colours to paint the squares and triangles.

5 Cut out a piece of thick card roughly 11cm (4¼in) square. Using the design shown on page 82 as a guide, start to build up the mosaic design. Secure the tiles with PVA glue and work line by line.

6 Continue adding lines of tiles to complete the design. Apply a coat of PVA glue all over the tiles using a large paintbrush. Leave to dry overnight.

Note When PVA glue is dry, it can be very difficult to remove, so wear an apron or old shirt to protect your clothes.

FURTHER IDEAS
You can make matching place mats and pot stands using this technique.

Seaside Pebble Frame

Small pebbles are great for making mosaics. You can sometimes find coloured ones on the beach, but you could paint the pebbles yourself if you could not find any. I have used white pebbles about the size of a pea and very small pebbles that have been painted after they have been glued down. Pearlescent paint has been used for a shimmering effect, which makes the picture frame look more colourful, but you can use any colour. Choose a frame with a very wide and flat border to give you plenty of space for your design, and use it to display your own drawing, painting or photograph.

YOU WILL NEED

Plain wooden frame
Selection of small pebbles
Newspaper • Carbon paper
Tracing paper • Masking tape
Pencil • Water-based paint
Paintbrush
PVA glue

 Transfer the patterns shown on page 83 on to your frame. Draw some waves in the background and then paint them, working from the top to the bottom.

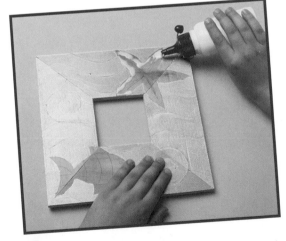

 Apply PVA glue around the edge of the starfish, over the fish's body and around the edge of the fish's tail.

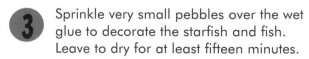 Sprinkle very small pebbles over the wet glue to decorate the starfish and fish. Leave to dry for at least fifteen minutes.

4 Tip the frame over a piece of newspaper to remove excess pebbles. These can be saved and used for another project.

5 Paint the small pebbles on the fish and the starfish in colours of your choice.

6 Apply glue to the centre of the starfish. Add stripes of glue to the fish's body and tail, and lines of glue following the shape of the waves. Press larger pebbles into the glue, then leave to dry overnight.

FURTHER IDEAS
Cover the top of a box, or make decorative pebble pictures using this technique.

Celestial Pot

All sorts of materials can be used to create a mosaic. Here broken eggshells are glued on to a plain terracotta plant pot. The theme is the sky above – one side shows a sun, the other a moon and star. For a small pot like this you will need the shells of three eggs. If your pot is larger, you will need more. Use the completed pot for an indoor plant, as the mosaic will not be weatherproof.

1 Wash the eggshells in warm water then place them on newspaper. Leave to dry.

2 Break the eggshells carefully into large pieces, then paint them with different colours. Leave to dry.

3 Transfer the patterns shown on page 83 on to your pot. Apply PVA glue to one of the areas of the design.

4 Break the eggshells into smaller pieces. Firmly press one of the pieces on to the wet glue to break the shell up further.

5 Use a cocktail stick to push the pieces of eggshell apart, leaving small gaps in between.

6 Continue applying different colours to your design. Finish by filling in around the design with more eggshells and leave to dry.

FURTHER IDEAS
Create a beautiful jewellery box by decorating a plain wooden box with brightly coloured eggshells.

Aztec Book Cover

This book cover is inspired by the wonderful colours of the
Aztecs. You can transform a cheap, plain, bound notebook
easily with the bold geometric pattern. Detailed mosaic
designs can take many hours to complete, but here the design
is very quick, as the mosaic is created on a printing block that
is then used to print a pattern over and over again. You can
use many colours on this block and print instant designs.

YOU WILL NEED

Plain book
High-density foam
Thick card • Scissors
Water-based paint
Paintbrush • PVA glue
Cord • Bead

 Cut high-density
foam into small
squares and
triangles, using
the design on
page 83 as a
rough guide.

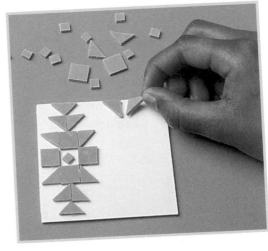

 Cut out a square of thick card,
roughly the size of the design.
Glue the foam pieces on to the
card using PVA glue, following
the lines of the design, to create
a printing block. Leave to dry.

3 Apply a thin layer of paint
to the foam squares and
triangles using a small
paintbrush and colours
of your choice.

4 Press the printing block on to the front of your book.

5 Repeat, applying more paint each time. Complete a stripe down one side of the book. Leave to dry.

6 Loop a length of cord around the book, then thread a tightly-fitting bead through to secure it.

FURTHER IDEAS
Create your own mosaic design using different shapes, then stamp the design on to a picture frame.

Patterns

You can trace the patterns on these pages straight from the book (step 1). Alternatively, you can make them larger or smaller on a photocopier if you wish, and then follow steps 2–4.

Ask an adult to help you enlarge the patterns on a photocopier.

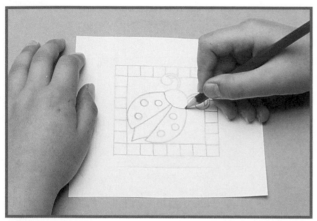

1 Place a piece of tracing paper over the pattern, then tape it down with small pieces of masking tape. Trace around the outline using a soft pencil.

2 Place carbon paper face down on the surface you want to transfer the design on to. Place the tracing or photocopy over the top and tape it in place.

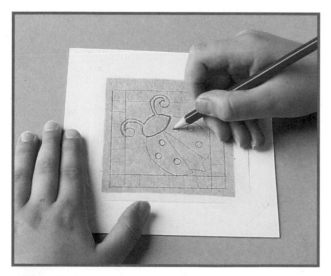

3 Trace over the outline with a pencil.

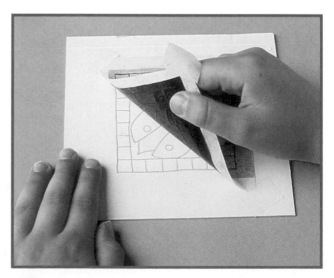

4 Remove the tracing paper and carbon paper to reveal the transferred image.

Patterns for the Insect Greetings Cards
featured on pages 60–61.

Patterns for the Knight in Armour
Picture featured on pages 64–65.

Pattern for the African Mask
featured on pages 62–63.

Pattern for the Indian Elephant Shoebag featured on pages 66–67.

Pattern for the Egyptian Eagle Necklace featured on pages 68–69.

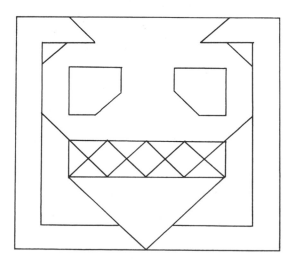

Pattern for the Grecian Coaster featured on pages 72–73.

Patterns for the Celestial Pot
featured on pages 76–77.

Pattern for the Aztec Book Cover
featured on pages 78–79.

Patterns for the Seaside Pebble Frame
featured on pages 74–75.

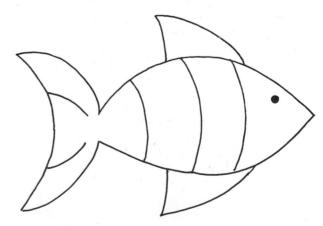

Papier Mâché

by Judy Balchin

Papier Mâché is a French term which means 'chewed or mashed paper'. It was first invented in China in the first part of the second century. The Chinese discovered that it was possible to make many items out of papier mâché – they created pots and even warrior helmets which they then covered with a varnish to make them hard-wearing and durable. Over time, mankind became more and more ambitious, and by the seventeenth century even a church was being built using papier mâché! In the following century, a man called Charles Ducrest drew up plans for making tables, bookcases and even houses, boats and bridges using either papier mâché on its own, or wood or iron structures covered in papier mâché.

Although you will not be making churches, houses or boats in this section, you will be able to have lots of fun with papier mâché – from making a simple photograph frame to modelling a cat. I have taken the inspiration for the items from past civilisations. You will be taken on a journey to discover Celtic and Indian decoration, Native American, Mexican and Gothic design, Egyptian, Aztec, Roman and African art.

There are two main ways of making papier mâché: layering and pulping. You will be using both methods in the projects in this section, sometimes combining both on one piece. Each project shows you a different way of using papier mâché and suggests how you can decorate your pieces.

If you are interested in recycling rubbish, then this section is definitely for you. Old newspapers, cardboard tubing and sweet wrappers are just a few of the things that you will be working with, so start hoarding! Before you throw anything away, ask yourself if it could be used in a papier mâché project. An old plastic bottle or cardboard box can spark off an amazing idea, so keep your eyes open. In particular, watch out for coloured papers, beads, feathers, string and foil papers . . . in fact anything that could be used to decorate your creations.

We all like to make things, but to make something totally unique has a special meaning. As you become more confident using papier mâché, I am sure you will come up with lots of your own ideas and designs. Be bold, experiment, but most of all, have lots of fun.

Techniques

Papier mâché is not a difficult craft, but it is worth reading through this techniques section carefully before you begin the projects.

Note Papier mâché is messy so it is best to cover your workspace with a large piece of newspaper. Alternatively, use polythene – this can be wiped down and used again.

Transferring a design on to cardboard

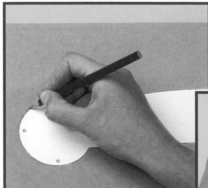

Patterns are provided at the end of the section. These can be enlarged on a photocopier. Cut around the photocopied pattern, then lay it on thin card or single corrugated cardboard and run round the edge with a pencil. Cut around the line with scissors.

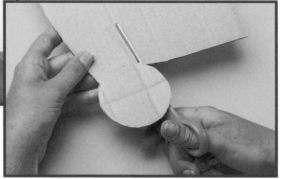

Double corrugated cardboard is much tougher than single, and it needs to be cut with a craft knife. Ask an adult to do this for you as craft knives are very sharp.

Preventing warping

Sometimes, papier mâché pieces made from a cardboard base can warp during the drying process. To prevent this, always give your base cardboard shape a coat of slightly diluted PVA glue.

Paste both sides of the cardboard then leave to dry naturally on a cooling rack, turning occasionally so that it dries evenly. When completely dry, the cardboard can be layered with newspaper strips (see opposite).

Note When PVA glue is dry, it can be very difficult to remove so wear an apron or old shirt to protect your clothes.

Mixing up the paste

Pour half a litre (one pint) of water into a bowl and sprinkle with wallpaper paste (the instructions on the packet will tell you how much to use). Stir the mixture well, leave it for fifteen minutes, then add a tablespoon of PVA glue to strengthen the paste.

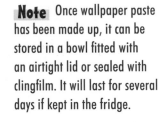

Note Once wallpaper paste has been made up, it can be stored in a bowl fitted with an airtight lid or sealed with clingfilm. It will last for several days if kept in the fridge.

Layering with newspaper strips

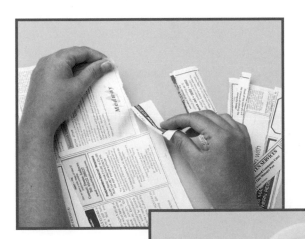

Layering involves pasting strips of newspaper with a mixture of wallpaper paste and PVA glue, and then sticking them on to a base. When dry, the pieces will be strong but light, and ready for decorating.

Tear small strips of newspaper for small structures, and larger strips for bigger items. Use your fingers to smear paste on to the strips of paper then press them on to your base so that they overlap each other. Smooth the strips down as you work.

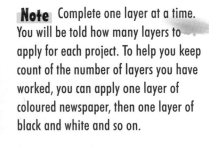

Note Complete one layer at a time. You will be told how many layers to apply for each project. To help you keep count of the number of layers you have worked, you can apply one layer of coloured newspaper, then one layer of black and white and so on.

Using paper pulp

Papier mâché pulp can be bought from art shops. It is a powdered paper which is mixed with water to create a modelling material. You can also make your own, as shown here. Once you have mixed up the pulp, it can be stored in a polythene bag in the fridge until needed.

1 Tear enough small pieces of newspaper to fill a mug when packed tightly.

 Place the pieces of newspaper in a bowl and cover with hot water. Leave to soak for three hours.

3 Transfer the soaked paper into a colander or sieve. Squeeze the pieces together so that the water runs out and the paper forms a mash.

4 Put the mash into a bowl and add a tablespoon of PVA glue and a tablespoon of wallpaper paste mixture (see page 87).

5 Mix everything together with your fingers.

Note When you have completed a pulped papier mâché project, leave it to dry naturally. The pulp shrinks as it dries and sometimes creates small splits or cracks in the surface. These can be disguised by smearing a little more paper pulp into them and allowing this to dry again.

Priming and painting

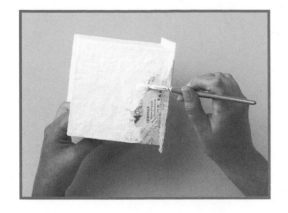

Priming means preparing a surface so that it can then be decorated with coloured paint. Use white emulsion paint to do this. You may need two coats to cover the newspaper print completely. Allow the first coat to dry before applying the second.

The projects in this book are decorated with acrylic paint as it covers well, is hard-wearing and does not need to be varnished. Once the white primer is dry, paint your finished object in colours of your choice.

Note All items painted with poster paint should be protected with a coat of varnish — you can use diluted PVA glue for this. If you do use poster paints, mix it with a little PVA glue before you apply it. This will prevent the paint from smearing when you varnish it.

Celtic Goblet

Celtic craftsmen were well-known for their metal work. The goblet in this project is made to look like metal, but it is actually made out of an old plastic drinks bottle. The surface is covered with pulp to create a textured surface which looks like beaten metal. It is decorated with metallic paint and glass droplets to create a container that is truly fit for a king! Remember that this goblet is purely decorative and can not be used to drink out of.

YOU WILL NEED

Plastic drinks bottle
Single corrugated cardboard
Paper pulp • Glass droplets
Metallic acrylic paint
Paintbrush • Palette • PVA glue
Scissors • Masking tape
Newspaper

1 Cut off the top third of a plastic drinks bottle.

2 Cut a circle of single corrugated cardboard approximately 6.5cm (2½in) in diameter. Use masking tape to attach the cardboard circle to the top of the bottle.

3 Cover the outside of the plastic bottle and the cardboard base with a layer of pulp.

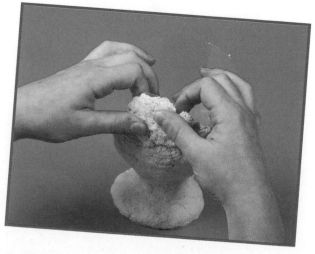

Note The pulp may dry on your fingers as you work. Keep a bowl of water next to you so that you can wet your fingers occasionally to stop this from happening.

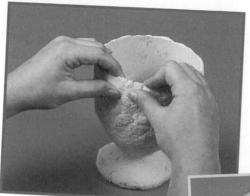

 4

Neaten the rim of the goblet by pressing the pulp onto the plastic edge.

5

While the pulp is still wet, put a blob of PVA glue on the back of eight glass droplets and then press them firmly into the pulp around the goblet. Leave to dry for forty-eight hours.

6

Paint the inside and outside of the goblet with metallic acrylic paint.

FURTHER IDEAS

Decorate your goblet using buttons or small pebbles instead of glass droplets.

Indian Frame

The shape of this Indian frame was inspired by the domed roof of the Taj Mahal, a beautiful tomb in India which was built by a Mogul Emperor for his wife. The decoration for the frame is based on Indian saris – these are made of brightly coloured cloth and metallic threads. I have used sweet wrappers and metallic paint in this project to transform a plain piece of cardboard into a frame to treasure.

YOU WILL NEED

Coloured foil sweet wrappers
Double corrugated cardboard
Thin card • Newspaper
Wallpaper paste • PVA glue • Paste brush
Metallic and coloured acrylic paint
Sponge • Palette • Pencil
Scissors • Craft knife • String
Masking tape

! Double corrugated cardboard needs to be cut with a craft knife. Ask an adult to do this for you as craft knives are very sharp.

 1 Photocopy and enlarge the pattern on page 109 (see page 108) then cut it out and place it on to a piece of double corrugated cardboard. Trace around the pattern with a pencil then cut out the cardboard frame.

 2 Paste both sides of the cardboard frame with PVA glue diluted with a little water. Leave to dry. Apply two layers of pasted newspaper strips to the front then leave to dry for a couple of hours.

3 Tear foil sweet wrappers into irregular shapes. Paste the back of each piece with PVA glue then press them on to the cardboard frame. Cover the front and the edges. Overlap the foil pieces on to the back. Leave to dry.

4 Pour a little metallic acrylic paint on to a palette. Dip a piece of sponge into the paint then dab it on to the outer and inner edges of the frame. Leave to dry.

5

Paint the back of the frame in a colour of your choice. Leave to dry. Cut out a piece of thin card, slightly bigger than the opening in the frame. Cut a wide 'v' shape in the top of the card. Tape the card over the opening, leaving the top un-taped – this will create a pocket for your picture or photograph.

FURTHER IDEAS
Create a different effect by decorating your frame with torn pieces of coloured tissue paper.

6 Tape a loop of string to the back of the frame for hanging, then leave to dry. Insert your picture or photograph.

Native American Headdress

A war bonnet decorated with eagle feathers is the mark of an experienced and respected warrior. The colourful headdress in this project is decorated with brightly coloured paints, beads and feathers. When you wear it, you will feel like the chief of your tribe.

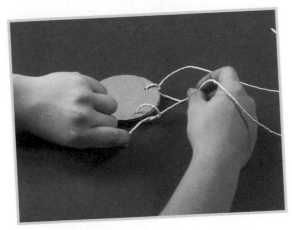

1 Use scissors to cut out the shape of the headdress shown on page 109 from single corrugated cardboard (see page 92). Pierce two holes in each disc shape with the end of a paintbrush. Thread a length of string through each hole and tie to secure.

2 Cover one side of the cardboard with pulp. Leave the corrugations along the top of the cardboard shape uncovered as you will later stick feathers into these. Add a little more pulp over the circular disk shapes. Roll out a sausage of pulp and press this along the headdress to create a raised zig-zag decoration.

3 Blow up a balloon to approximately the same size as your head. Use masking tape to attach the balloon to a small bowl. Tie the headdress around the balloon and leave to dry for forty-eight hours.

94

4

Prime the headdress with white emulsion. When dry, decorate with zig-zags and dots of coloured acrylic paint.

FURTHER IDEAS
Paint the headband with earthy colours and use natural feathers for a different effect.

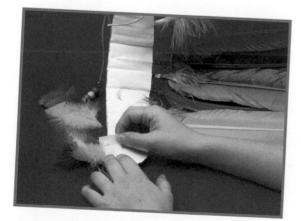

5 Sponge the lengths of string with coloured paint. When dry, thread the strings at the bottom with coloured beads. Leave the strings at the side un-beaded, so you can tie it around your head.

6 Push large coloured feathers into the holes along the top of the corrugated card, then tape two small feathers down each side.

95

Mexican Bowl

YOU WILL NEED

Selection of coloured beads
60cm (24in) of leather thong
Bowl • Clingfilm • Paper pulp
Newspaper • White emulsion paint
Coloured acrylic paint
Paintbrush • Palette
Cooling rack

The inspiration for this bright little bowl comes from Mexico. In fact, the art of pot-making originated from the Mexican area as there was a lot of clay in the soil. Mexicans use bright colours and geometric designs to decorate their craft work. In this project, paper pulp is used to make a textured bowl. You can use any bowl as a mould for this project (ceramic, plastic or glass) and it does not matter what size it is. Remember that the finished papier mâché bowl is intended to be decorative – you cannot eat out of it!

Line the inside of a bowl with clingfilm. Press paper pulp into the bowl with your fingers. When it is about 1cm (½in) thick, smooth the surface with your fingers.

2 Use the end of a paintbrush to make holes around the bowl. Try to make the spaces between the holes roughly equal. Leave to dry for three hours.

3 Carefully lift the pulp shell out of the bowl using the clingfilm. Place on a cooling rack then leave to dry for at least twenty-four hours.

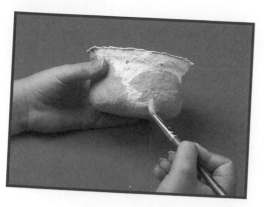

4

Prime the bowl with two coats of white emulsion paint. Leave to dry. Paint the outside of the bowl with coloured acrylic paint. Leave to dry.

5 Paint the inside of the bowl a different colour. Leave to dry.

6

Tie a knot in the length of thong and attach three beads. Thread it through one of the holes in the bowl. Tie a knot on the inside then cut off the end of the thong. Repeat around the bowl using the rest of the thong.

FURTHER IDEAS
Use a needle and cotton to thread dried melon or sunflower seeds on to your bowl.

Gothic Mirror

Gothic architecture sparked off the idea for this mirror. If you visit an old church and look at the pointed arches and carved stonework you will soon see the similarities. The mirror in this project is created using a mirror tile on a cardboard base. I have covered the cardboard with paper pulp to create a stone brickwork effect.

YOU WILL NEED
Mirror tile
Double corrugated cardboard
Paper pulp • Newspaper • PVA glue
Wallpaper paste • Paste brush
Natural-coloured acrylic paint
Paintbrush • Palette • Ruler
Masking tape • Soft cloth
Cooling rack

1 Cut out the frame shape shown on page 108 from double corrugated card (see page 92). Coat both sides with diluted PVA glue then allow to dry on a cooling rack.

2 Apply two layers of pasted newspaper strips to the front and back of the frame. Leave to dry for four hours.

3 Apply PVA glue to the back of the mirror and then press it into place on the frame.

4 Press paper pulp on to the front and edges of the cardboard frame. Smooth the pulp with your fingers as you work.

5

While the pulp is still wet, use the long edge of a ruler to press horizontal lines into the pulp. Use the short edge of the ruler to create vertical lines. This will give the effect of stone brickwork. Leave to dry for forty-eight hours.

6 Paint the frame with natural-coloured paint then polish the mirror with a soft cloth.

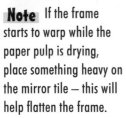 **Note** If the frame starts to warp while the paper pulp is drying, place something heavy on the mirror tile — this will help flatten the frame.

FURTHER IDEAS
Make the mirror frame Norman rather than Gothic by cutting out a rounded arch.

Egyptian Cat

The Ancient Egyptians worshipped the cat goddess, Bastet, and made bronze cat figures dedicated to her. Bastet represented the power of the sun to ripen crops. This project uses a plastic bottle and a polystyrene ball as a base for re-creating Bastet. Pulp is used to model her features and, once painted, she is sponged with metallic paint to make her look like a real goddess.

YOU WILL NEED
Plastic drinks bottle
Polystyrene ball • Ribbon
Paper pulp • Newspaper
Coloured and metallic acrylic paint
Palette • Sponge • Paintbrush
PVA glue • Paste brush
Masking tape

1 Remove the bottle cap and place the polystyrene ball on top of the bottle. Tape the ball into place with long strips of masking tape. Press the tape flat on to the bottle to create a smooth finish.

2 Cover the polystyrene ball with a layer of paper pulp. Build up the nose then model two triangles of pulp to create the ears. Smooth the pulp with your fingers as you work.

3 Work down the bottle, covering it with pulp. Build up the front legs and feet then the hind legs and feet using pulp. Neaten the base of the bottle then leave to dry for two days.

4 Paint the cat with coloured acrylic paint. Leave to dry. Paint in the eyes and nose in a darker colour.

5 Paint in the collar with coloured and metallic paint then leave to dry. Glue on a strip of ribbon around the top of the collar.

6 Pour a little metallic paint on to a palette. Lightly sponge the cat all over.

FURTHER IDEAS
Look for a picture of the Egyptian god, Anubis, who is represented as a jackal. Try creating a model of its head.

Aztec Necklace

Aztec craftsmen made beautiful jewellery. They considered jade to be their most precious stone, but they also used onyx, rock crystal and turquoise. The necklace in this project is made out of pulp which has been decorated with string, foil and metallic paint.

YOU WILL NEED
Foil • String
Paper pulp • Newspaper
Clingfilm • Cardboard
Coloured and metallic acrylic paint
Paintbrush • Sponge
PVA glue • Paste brush
Masking tape
Cooling rack

1 Tape a piece of clingfilm over a piece of card so that it is stretched tight.

2 Model a rectangle and a triangle of pulp then press each shape on to the clingfilm, flattening them with your fingers.

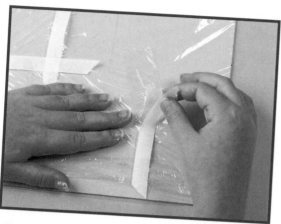

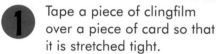

3 Press string into each pulp shape to create swirling patterns.

4 Use the end of a paintbrush to create two holes in the top corners and one in the bottom of the rectangular piece. Make one hole at the top of the triangle. Leave to dry for an hour. Carefully remove the shapes from the clingfilm then lay them on a cooling rack and leave to dry for a further twelve hours.

6

Sponge a length of string with metallic paint. Cut off a short piece and use this to link the rectangle and triangle together. Tie two longer pieces of string on to the rectangle so that you can do the necklace up.

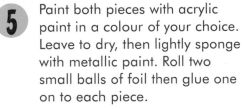

5 Paint both pieces with acrylic paint in a colour of your choice. Leave to dry, then lightly sponge with metallic paint. Roll two small balls of foil then glue one on to each piece.

FURTHER IDEAS

Model round pieces of pulp and attach earring clips to the back to make earrings. Thread round shapes with string to create a bracelet.

Roman Box

Roman city houses were often plain on the outside, but on the inside they were painted with scenes from mythology or the countryside. Romans covered their floors with mosaics (pictures and patterns made up from small pieces of stone). This project shows you how to make a simple mosaic box using cardboard, paint and a potato stamp. I have varnished the finished piece with diluted PVA glue to make it look shiny.

YOU WILL NEED
Potato
Single corrugated cardboard
Newspaper • Wallpaper paste
Vegetable knife • Chopping board
White emulsion paint
Coloured acrylic paint
Paintbrush • Palette • PVA glue
Paste brush • Masking tape
Scissors

1 Cut out four 12cm (4¾in) and two 14cm (5½in) squares from single corrugated cardboard. Now cut out one 11cm (4¼in) and one 4cm (1½in) square. Tape the four 12cm (4¾in) squares together with masking tape to form the sides of the box. Tape one 14cm (5½in) square to one end to create a base.

2 To make a lid, glue the 11cm (4¼in) square to the centre of the remaining 14cm (5½in) square. Leave to dry. Turn over and pierce through the centre of the larger square with the end of a paintbrush. Apply a blob of glue to the hole then push a corner of the 4cm (1½in) square into the hole. Secure with small pieces of masking tape.

3 Coat the box and lid with diluted PVA glue. Leave to dry then apply two layers of pasted newspaper strips to the box. Leave to dry for four hours. Prime the box with two coats of white emulsion. Leave to dry.

4 Cut a 1cm (½in) wide chip shape from a potato. Dab it into acrylic paint then use it to stamp the sides of the box.

(!)

It is best to cut the potato on a chopping board. Get an adult to help you do this as vegetable knives are very sharp.

5 Stamp three rows of squares around the lid then paint the handle.

6 Paint the rim of the base and the inside of the box. Leave to dry then apply a coat of diluted PVA glue to varnish the outside of the box and the lid.

FURTHER IDEAS

Cut triangular and rectangular shaped potato shapes and use these to stamp a different design on to your box.

African Pencil Pot

The inspiration for this project comes from African drums. I have used cardboard tubing to recreate the cylindrical drum shapes and have decorated the pencil pot with colours typical of African art. It is best to use different sizes of cardboard tubing. You can make a simple pencil pot using just a few tubes, or you can use lots to create a more complicated one.

YOU WILL NEED

Cardboard tubing • Thin card
Newspaper • Wallpaper paste
PVA glue • Coloured acrylic paint
White emulsion paint • Sponge
Small paintbrush • Palette
Masking tape • Scissors
Pencil

Cut out five different lengths of cardboard tubing. Tape the tubes together, making sure that the bases are level. Place the tubes on a piece of thin card and draw around the bases. Cut around this shape then attach it to the bottom of the tubes using masking tape.

Prime the pencil pot with white emulsion paint then leave to dry. Apply a coat of coloured acrylic paint. When dry, paint coloured lines down each tube and a zig-zag border around the base. Leave to dry.

Apply two layers of newspaper strips over the pencil pot then allow to dry for four hours.

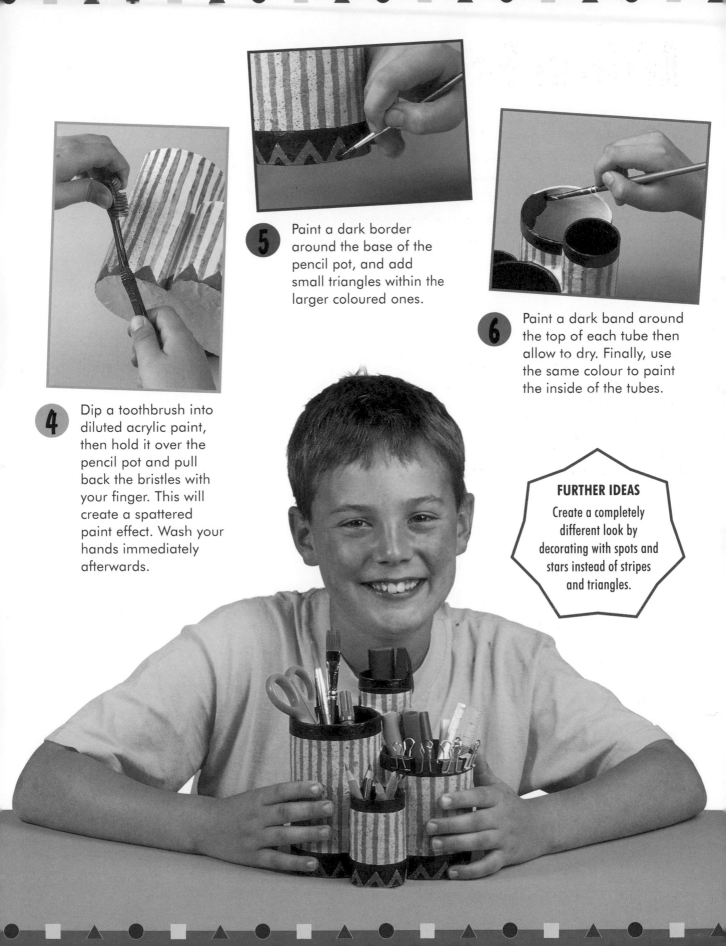

5 Paint a dark border around the base of the pencil pot, and add small triangles within the larger coloured ones.

6 Paint a dark band around the top of each tube then allow to dry. Finally, use the same colour to paint the inside of the tubes.

4 Dip a toothbrush into diluted acrylic paint, then hold it over the pencil pot and pull back the bristles with your finger. This will create a spattered paint effect. Wash your hands immediately afterwards.

FURTHER IDEAS
Create a completely different look by decorating with spots and stars instead of stripes and triangles.

Patterns

You can photocopy the patterns on these pages and then transfer the designs on to cardboard (see page 86). Use them the size that they appear here, or make them larger or smaller on a photocopier if you wish.

> **(!)** Get an adult to help you photocopy the patterns.

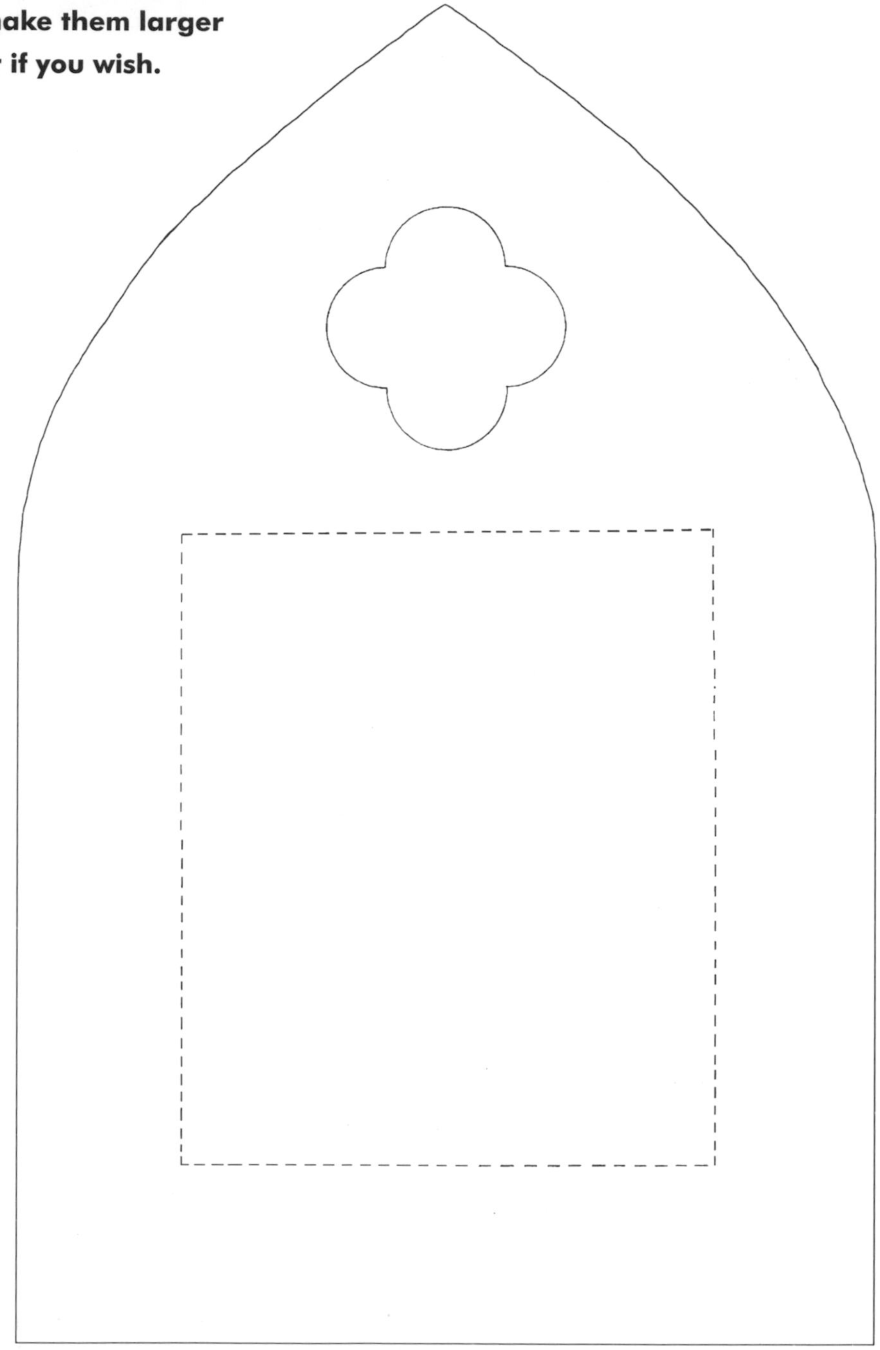

Pattern for the Gothic Mirror
featured on pages 98–99.

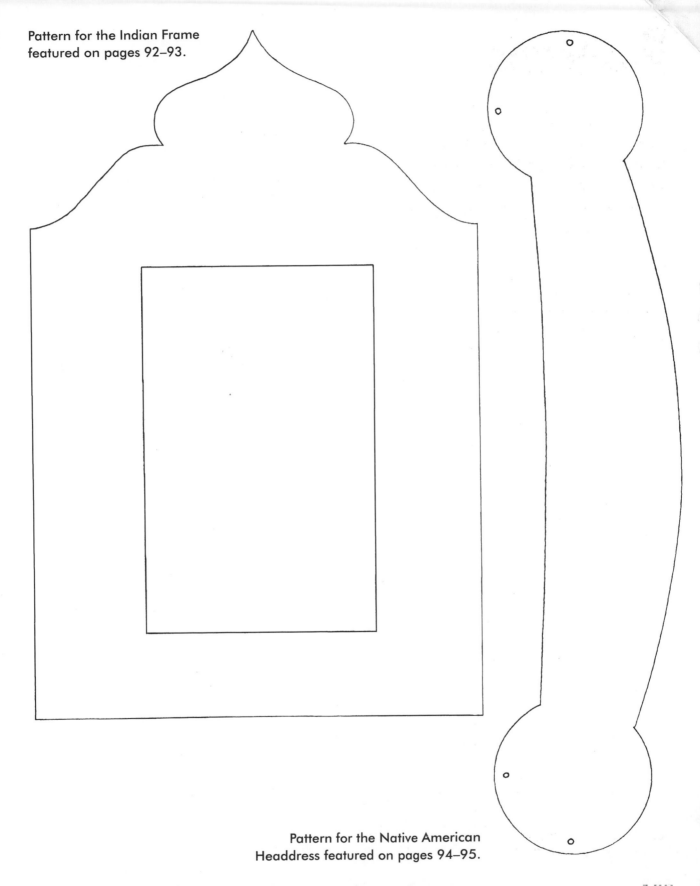

Pattern for the Indian Frame
featured on pages 92–93.

Pattern for the Native American
Headdress featured on pages 94–95.

Origami

by Clive Stevens

It is generally believed that paper was invented in China around the first century AD, and the Chinese soon began to fold the new material into decorative shapes. When paper was introduced to Japan in the sixth century AD by Buddhist monks, it rapidly became an important part of their culture. Paper was used as part of many religious ceremonies, and even as a building material. It was the Japanese who turned paper folding into an art, which in Japan is as important as painting and sculpture. Origami comes from the Japanese words for folding, *ori*, and paper, *kami*.

The Japanese passed on their paper folding designs by word of mouth; many were passed down from mother to daughter. In the early days, paper was too expensive to be used for fun, so paper folding was done only for important ceremonies. Paper butterflies were made to decorate the cups for *sake* (rice wine) used at Japanese weddings.

By the seventeenth century, paper had become less expensive, and origami had become a popular pastime in Japan. The first origami books with diagrams and instructions were published in the early eighteenth century.

Today, master paper folders can be found all over the world. Folding techniques have improved so much that they would have astounded the ancient Japanese who invented origami.

In this section, you will learn how to make good, crisp folds so that your paper will hold the right shapes. Follow the instructions carefully, and this is all you need to know to make some simple but very effective projects.

In origami, many different shapes can be made from a few simple bases. The Origami Bases chapter on pages 114–115 shows you how to make two of these bases, and once you have mastered folding these, you are ready to make some very impressive projects!

Don't worry if your folding doesn't work the first time. Go over the instructions and pictures again carefully, and you will soon find where you went wrong.

You hardly need any materials to do origami, and it is easy to become hooked. After a few tries, you will learn the folds off by heart, and then all you need is a piece of paper to produce impressive designs that will amaze your friends!

Techniques

Folding in half

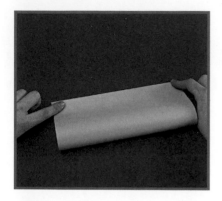

1 Fold the bottom corners upwards to meet the top corners. This will make a horizontal fold.

2 Make a crease in the middle. Press with your finger from the middle to the edge, then from the middle to the other edge. Make sure the corners stay together.

3 Reinforce the crease by pressing it with your fingernail.

Folding diagonally

Start with a square piece of paper. Lift up one corner and meet it up with the corner diagonally opposite to it. Make a crease in the middle of the paper and work out from the middle to the sides. This makes a diagonal fold.

Folding at an angle

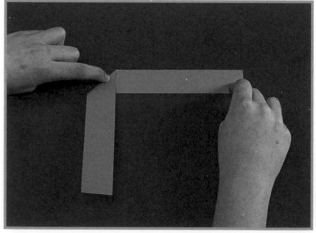

Lay a strip of paper horizontally. Fold part of the strip downwards so that the edges of the strip make a right angle, like the corner of a square.

Reverse Folding (internal)

Reverse folding means that you push a fold until it folds in the opposite direction. A valley fold (which dips downwards) becomes a mountain fold (which points upwards), and vice versa. This internal reverse fold is used for the Flapping Bird project on pages 132–133.

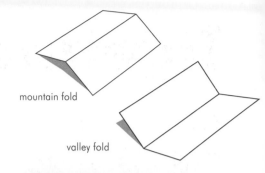

mountain fold

valley fold

 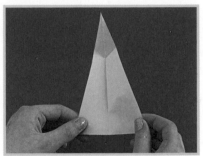 

1 Fold a square piece of paper in half diagonally. Fold the top corner down as shown and crease it sharply.

2 Open the paper up slightly. Pull the top point towards you. Reverse the mountain fold in the middle of the point, making it a valley fold.

3 Remake the diagonal fold and open it up to show the point with its valley fold.

Reverse Folding (external)

This type of external reverse fold is used for the Paper Penguin project on pages 120–121.

1 Take a square piece of paper and fold it diagonally. Fold down the top point as shown and crease firmly.

2 Open up with the diagonal mountain fold facing towards you. Fold the top point towards you. Reverse the fold in the middle of the point. Now remake the diagonal fold, so that the point comes down on the outside of the diagonal fold.

Origami Bases

Many origami designs come from a few simple bases. Here are two bases which can lead to all sorts of different projects.

Bird Base

This base is used to make the Flapping Bird project on page 132. Steps 1 to 3 also start off the Folded Flower project on page 128.

1 Take a square of paper. Fold the square diagonally. Crease it firmly and open. Fold on the other diagonal, crease and open. Turn the paper over so that your diagonal folds are mountain folds, as shown above.

2 Now fold up the bottom two corners to meet the top two corners and fold the paper in half horizontally. Crease, unfold, and then fold in half the other way to make a cross shape. Turn the paper over and place it as shown, so that the horizontal folds are mountain folds, and the diagonal folds are valley folds that dip down.

3 Hold the edges of a horizontal fold as shown. Move your hands in together until the paper forms a square. There should be two flaps on either side of the square as shown.

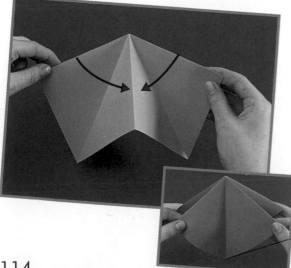

open end

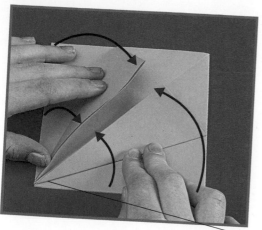

open end

open end

 4 Fold the front flaps, bringing the edges in to the middle. Make sure the open end of the shape is at the bottom as shown.

5 Turn over and repeat on the other side.

Rocket Base

This is used in the Space Rocket project on pages 130–131 and the Blow-up Box on pages 134–135.

1 Start making the Bird Base, but only go as far as Step 2. Turn the paper over so that the diagonal folds are mountain folds and the horizontal folds are valley folds. Fold one of the diagonal folds and hold it by the corners. Push your hands downwards to form a triangle.

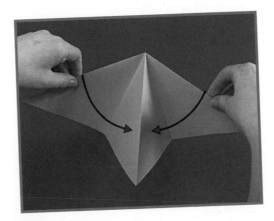

2 The triangle should have two flaps on either side, like the square made in step 3 of the Bird Base.

Note If your origami bases have not turned out right, check these things:
• Make sure your folds are sharply creased.
• If your diagonal folds are mountain folds, your horizontal folds should be valley folds.
• Make sure the open end of the shape is at the bottom.

Layered Fan

Many people have learnt to make a simple fan by folding a piece of paper into a concertina shape. This may have been your first introduction to paper folding! However, folding this way can lead to uneven folds and an untidy finished fan. This is an origami fan, made from basic valley and mountain folds. This method means that you fold the paper so that it is divided equally.

YOU WILL NEED
Three different coloured papers:
10 x 30cm (4 x 11¾in)
12 x 30cm (4¾ x 11¾in)
14 x 30cm (5½ x 11¾in)

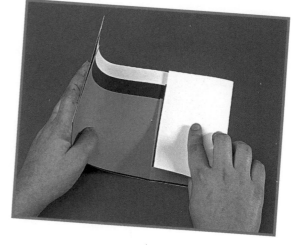

1 Place all three pieces of paper together as shown. Fold them in half and unfold.

2 Fold the right and left edges in to the centre line.

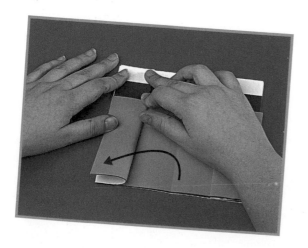

3 Take one of the edges that you have folded in to the middle, and fold it back to the new edge. Repeat the other side as shown.

Fold in half, bringing the double outside edges together.

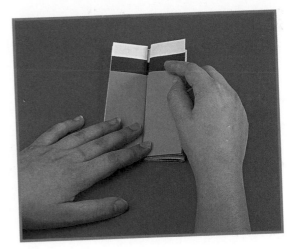

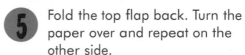

Fold the top flap back. Turn the paper over and repeat on the other side.

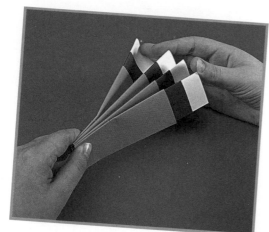

Open up and pinch at the bottom to form a multicoloured fan.

FURTHER IDEAS

Make fans from patterned origami paper, wrapping paper, or even beautiful Japanese handmade papers.

Secrets Folder

This handy folder is made using simple folds and also a tuck fold. It can be any size you want, from a tiny purse for loose change, to a folder like the one shown here, for larger secrets! Remember that the folder you end up with will be much smaller than the piece of paper you start with. You need to cut down an A2 size piece of paper to make a folder as big as the one shown in these photographs. What you hide in your secrets folder is up to you!

YOU WILL NEED
Coloured or patterned paper
30 x 50cm (12 x 20in)

1 Place the paper, shiny side down and fold in half horizontally. Unfold. Fold the two top corners in to the centre line.

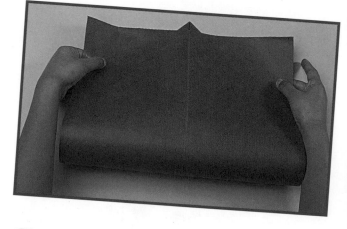

2 Fold the bottom edge up to the point at the top.

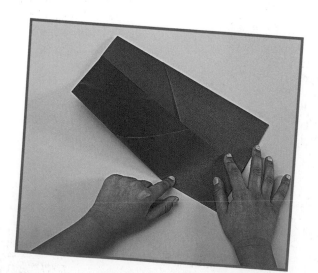

3 Now fold the outside edges in to the centre fold.

Fold the bottom edge to the top of the diagonal folds.

Tuck the flap into the front pocket.

Fold the point down to form the front flap of the secrets folder.

FURTHER IDEAS

Try using metallic or patterned papers, or decorate a piece of paper yourself using paints or felt tip pens before folding.

Paper Penguin

Origami paper with black on one side and white on the other works perfectly for this project. Using very few folds, you can create something that stands up like a real penguin. Penguins are some of the most sociable of all birds – they like to swim and feed in groups, so why not make a whole group of penguins and a paper pool for them to go fishing in?

YOU WILL NEED
One 10cm (4in) square piece of paper, black on one side and white on the other.

1 Take your square piece of paper. Fold it diagonally in half with the white on the inside to make a crease, then unfold. Turn the paper over. Take a corner at one end of the diagonal fold, and fold it up 2½cm (1in) as shown. Crease sharply.

2 Reverse the diagonal fold so that the white is on the outside, to make the shape shown.

3 Fold the top point down to 1½cm (½in) from the bottom fold, and crease. Turn the paper over and repeat. This step is like making the wings on a paper aeroplane.

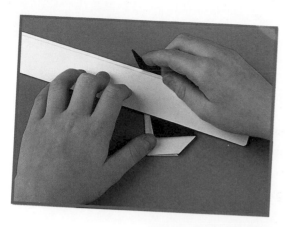

Place a ruler over the shape and fold the point down against the edge of a ruler at the angle shown. Remove the ruler and crease.

Open up slightly and pull the point towards you, making an external reverse fold as shown on page 113. This will make the penguin's head point downwards.

Crease the penguin again so that it is completely flat and open it up to reveal the finished penguin.

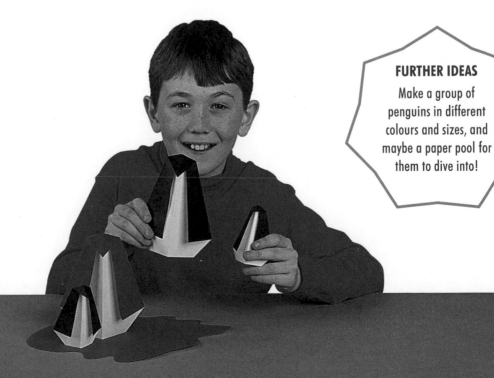

FURTHER IDEAS

Make a group of penguins in different colours and sizes, and maybe a paper pool for them to dive into!

Picture Frame

This simple origami frame is the perfect place to put one of your drawings, or a favourite photograph. Use thin card instead of paper, as this will make a stronger frame. The picture that goes inside this frame can be up to 14.5cm (5¾in) square, but don't forget that only a 10.5cm (4in) square in the middle will show.

YOU WILL NEED
Square of brightly coloured thin card,
30 x 30cm
(11¾ x 11¾in)

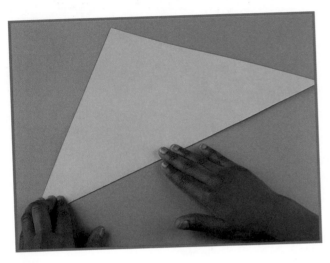

1 Fold the square diagonally corner to corner.

2 Open up and repeat on the other two corners.

3 Open up again. Your diagonal folds should be valley folds. Fold one corner down to the centre. Fold the other corners down to the centre.

4

Turn the paper over and again fold all corners down to the centre.

5

Turn the base over and fold all the points out to their corners.

6

Measure your picture frame. Draw a picture or find a photograph this size, remembering that the corners will be hidden by the frame. Slide the picture into the frame.

FURTHER IDEAS
Fold only as far as step 4 to make a drinks mat. Cover the mat in plastic to make it spill-proof.

Japanese Card

People have been sending one another greetings cards for hundreds of years. The first ones celebrated holidays or religious festivals, but nowadays they are sent for all kinds of reasons. Handmade cards are even more special than shop-bought ones. This Japanese greetings card has contrasting shades of the same colour to make it eye-catching. You open the flaps and write your message inside.

YOU WILL NEED
Two pieces of contrasting coloured paper, 23.5cm (9in) square

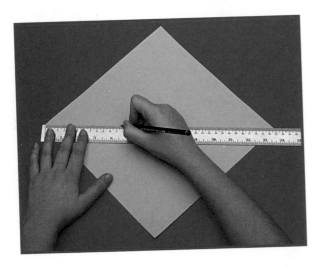

1 Put the squares of paper one on top of the other. Measure across the diagonal and mark it in to thirds of 11cm (4¼in) each.

2 Fold the corner along the diagonal. Fold on your first mark, up to your second mark.

3 Unfold. Turn the paper round and fold the opposite corner up to your first fold.

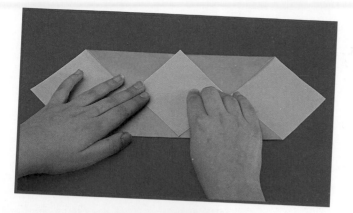

Fold one corner up to the top edge. Take the opposite corner out from under the top flap and fold it down to the bottom edge.

Fold one side in to cover the central light-coloured square. Fold the other side in as well.

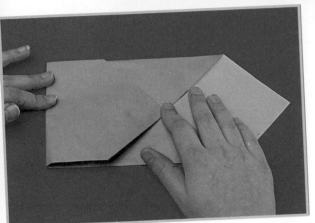

Fold the triangular flap out to the outside edge and repeat the other side.

FURTHER IDEAS

Create a traditional Japanese card from glossy black and red paper.

Obi Bookmark

This traditional folding technique looks like the sash or *obi* worn round a Japanese kimono. Use bright, contrasting colours to give your bookmark a modern look. You need long strips of paper to start with, so make sure you cut them from an A2 size sheet. Once you have mastered the overlapping technique, you will be able to make a variety of bookmarks in different lengths and colours. They make the ideal gift for a friend who likes reading.

YOU WILL NEED

Two strips of paper in contrasting colours, 54 x 3cm (21¼ x 1¼in)
Scissors
Ruler

26cm (10¼in) from left

Put one strip on top of the other. Fold the strips at an angle, as shown on page 112. The fold should come 26cm (10¼in) from the left-hand end of the strips.

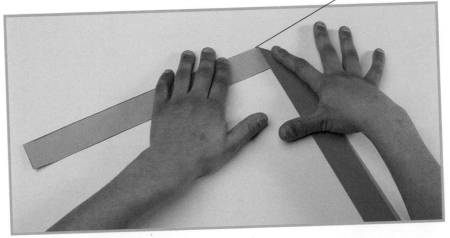

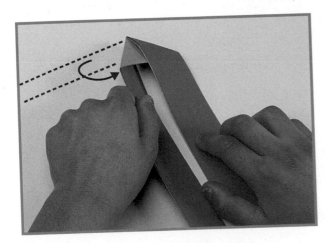

Fold the left-hand strips under at an angle. The strips should run parallel with the right-hand strips.

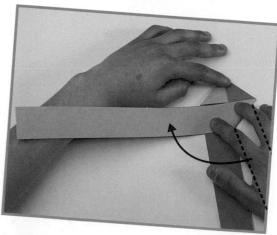

Fold the right-hand strip at an angle as shown.

126

 4

Slip the top right-hand strips under the left-hand strips.

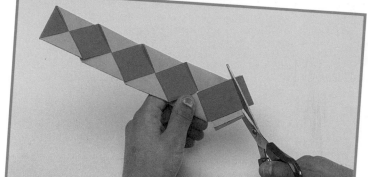

5 Repeat steps 2, 3 and 4. Carry on doing this until four squares have been formed.

6 Fold the excess under neatly or trim the ends using scissors.

FURTHER IDEAS

Use contrasting papers: weave textured and glossy paper or patterned and plain paper together.

Folded Flower

This origami flower starts out as a square, but with a few folds it turns in to a flower shape, and curling the ends of the petals gives it a natural beauty. Why not make lots of flowers in different colours, with straws or pipe cleaners for stems. Then you can arrange them in a vase or bouquet.

YOU WILL NEED
Square of brightly coloured paper, 10 x 10cm (4 x 4in)
Pencil or cocktail stick

1 Fold the square diagonally. Crease it firmly and open up. Then fold it on the other diagonal and open up the paper as shown above. Your diagonal folds should be mountain folds.

2 Fold up the bottom two corners to meet the top two corners and make a horizontal fold. Crease, unfold and then fold the paper in half the other way. Now your horizontal folds are mountain folds and your diagonal folds are valley folds.

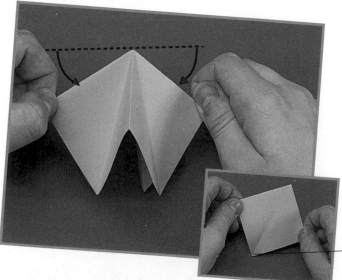

3 Hold the ends of a horizontal fold with both hands as shown, moving your hands together until the paper forms a square with two flaps on each side.

open end

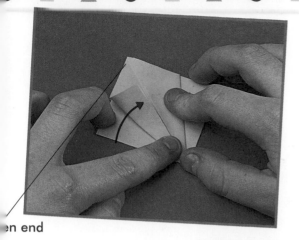

 Turn the square the other way up so that the open point is at the top. Fold the front flaps as shown, bringing the edges into the middle. Crease firmly. Turn over and repeat on the other side.

open end

 open end

5

Unfold one of the small flaps and reverse the fold so that it becomes a valley fold instead of a mountain fold. Repeat with the other three flaps.

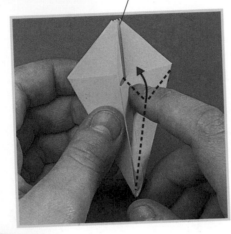

6 Open out the flower. Using a pencil or a cocktail stick, roll the tops of all four points down to create the natural curl of a petal.

FURTHER IDEAS
Make much bigger flowers, and then make smaller flowers without curling the petals. These make centres for the big flowers.

Space Rocket

This rocket is made from silver metallic origami paper that is white on the other side. It has legs that point outwards at an angle, so that it can stand up on its own, ready for take-off! Once you have mastered the Rocket Base, you are ready to fold and launch your own rocket – or maybe a whole fleet of spaceships!

YOU WILL NEED
Square of metallic paper, 21 x 21cm (8¼ x 8¼in)

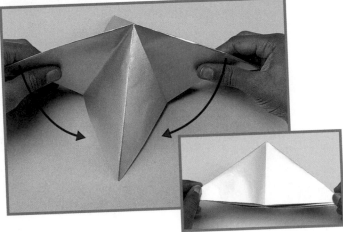

1 First make the Rocket Base as shown on page 115. Make sure that the shiny side of the paper is on the outside when you make your diagonal folds and on the inside when you make the horizontal folds. Hold the edges of a diagonal mountain fold and bring your hands in to make the triangle shape shown, with two flaps on each side.

2 Fold the outer edges in to the middle as shown. Turn the paper over and repeat.

3 Fold the outer corners to the middle. Turn the paper over and repeat on the other side.

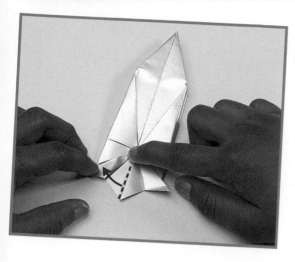

4

Fold the bottom points out at an angle as shown.

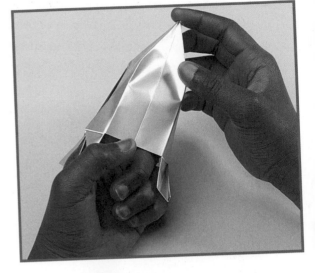

5

Turn over and repeat.

6 Carefully open up the rocket by placing your finger inside.

FURTHER IDEAS
Leave the rocket flat as in step 5 and glue it on to a greetings card.

Flapping Bird

This bird is a variation of the traditional origami crane, a bird that is a Japanese symbol for peace. The crane is also the symbol for many international origami societies. This version is simpler, but if you hold it in the right place, it actually flaps its wings. Once you have got the hang of the Bird Base shown on pages 114–115, you will be ready to fold this impressive project to amaze all your friends.

YOU WILL NEED
Square piece of paper, 24.5cm² (9¾in²)

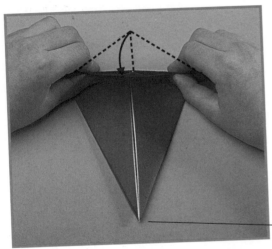

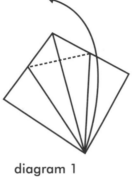

diagram 1

open end

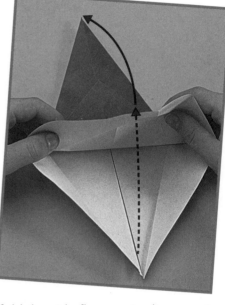

1 Start with the Bird Base, with the open end at the bottom. Fold the smaller triangle down, crease and fold back to its original position.

2 Unfold the side flaps as in diagram 1. Fold the bottom point up, covering the small triangle from step 1. Fold the point right up to the top, reversing the diagonal folds to form a diamond. Turn over and repeat this step on the back to make the shape shown in diagram 2.

3

Fold the top flap on the right over to the left. Turn the paper over and repeat, folding the top right flap only to the left.

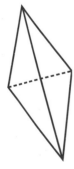

diagram 2

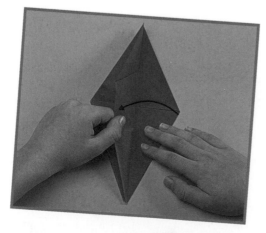

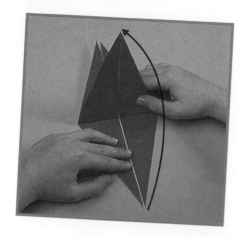

 Fold the bottom flap up. Turn over and repeat.

5 Pull the hidden points in the middle out and down, and crease them in the position shown. These will make the bird's head and tail.

6 Fold the head down as shown, unfold it then make an internal reverse fold as shown at the top of page 113. To make your bird flap its wings, hold the two bottom points and gently pull them apart.

FURTHER IDEAS
Make birds in different sizes and colours, attach thread to their bodies and hang them from a coat hanger to make a mobile.

Blow-up Box

This classic Japanese origami design just looks like an interesting shape when you have finished folding it. However, if you blow into it, it inflates to make a three-dimensional box. Fold the Rocket Base first, and with a few simple folds and some clever tucks, you will soon have an origami shape with a built-in surprise!

1 Begin with the Rocket Base on page 115. Fold the bottom corners of the two front flaps up to the top point.

2 Turn the paper over and repeat on the other side.

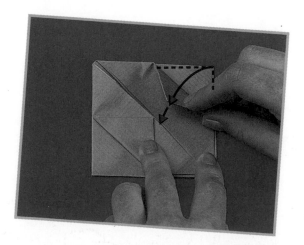

3 Bring the two outer corners of the front flaps in to the centre and crease as shown.

 4

Turn the paper over and repeat.

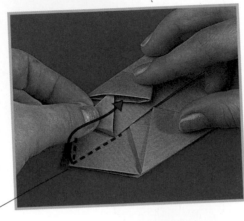 **5**

Make sure the loose points are at the top and tuck the front two loose points in the triangle pockets as far as you can. They will not go all the way in. Turn the paper over and repeat.

 Top

 **6**

Hold the paper lightly between your fingers and thumbs. Put the open end to your mouth and blow into the opening. The box should now inflate.

FURTHER IDEAS

Make boxes in bright metallic colours and hang them up as Christmas decorations, or make red lanterns for Chinese New Year.

Handmade Cards   by Tamsin Carter

Commercial greetings cards are sent for all sorts of reasons: to wish someone a happy birthday, or good luck; to celebrate a festival such as Christmas or New Year; to say thank you, congratulations, or just hello. A greetings card tells someone that you are thinking of them and that you care, and it gives them a picture to display in their home. Just think how much more special a handmade card is, because you have created it yourself and chosen the message personally.

People all over the world have been sending each other hand-decorated messages and cards for hundreds of years, probably since paper became widely available. The oldest known Valentine's card was made in the 1400s and is in the British Museum. Printed cards came later, in the nineteenth century, and were mainly for celebrating holidays or religious festivals.

In this section I show you how to make a variety of different cards using a range of materials including felt, pipe cleaners, beads and even wobbly plastic eyes! Do not worry if you think you cannot draw very well, as there are patterns in the back of the book to help you. I have also included a section on page 158 which shows you easy methods of transferring designs and scoring and folding card. There are lots of fun techniques to try like paint spattering, sewing and collage.

Inspiration can come from all sorts of sources. I usually think of the person I am making the card for, and that gets me started. In this book there are cards inspired by space, nature, musical instruments, dinosaurs, sport, famous artists and ancient wonders. Once you have chosen your subject, you can investigate it further by searching for information in libraries, galleries and museums and on the internet.

Nature is a very good place to find inspiration. You can collect leaves, sticks and flowers to make a collage, or look at the weather and the amazing effects it has on our world. Sometimes the materials themselves can be inspiring: just laying them out in front of you can be enough to trigger an idea and get you started.

Most importantly remember there are no rules; the more you experiment and dare to try something new, the more wonderful your cards will be. A card can be simple or complicated, take an hour to make or just five minutes. A greetings card is very special, it is a gift and a message all in one. Enjoy making them and people will enjoy receiving them.

Nazca Birds

In the 1930s, pilots were flying over the desert in Peru in South America when they saw giant drawings on the ground. There was a monkey the size of a football pitch, a lizard twice that length, a spider, fish, birds and insects. It is thought that they were made by the Nazca Indians around two thousand years ago, but nobody knows why. Have a look at them in a library or on the internet and try to imagine why they were made and how. This card is inspired by one of the Nazca drawings, of a large bird called a condor.

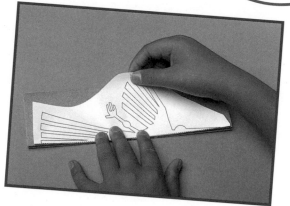

Ask an adult to help you to photocopy the design.

2 Photocopy the design on page 160. Cut round it roughly and stick it on to the folded sandpaper with a glue stick. Make sure that the dotted line that runs down one side of the pattern is up against the outer folds. Don't worry if the bird's wings overlap the edge.

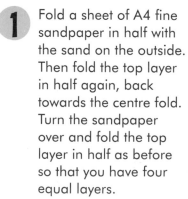

1 Fold a sheet of A4 fine sandpaper in half with the sand on the outside. Then fold the top layer in half again, back towards the centre fold. Turn the sandpaper over and fold the top layer in half as before so that you have four equal layers.

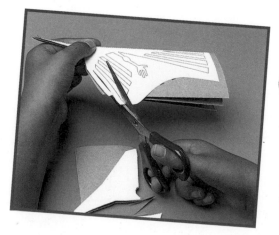

3 Carefully cut out the bird shape. Make sure you do not cut off the ends of the feathers that have dotted lines. They should extend to meet the fold.

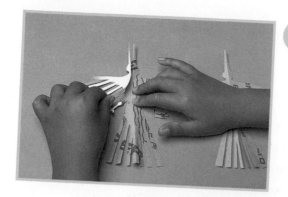

4 Open out the sandpaper to reveal two condors joined at the wings. Peel off the photocopied pattern. Do not worry if some parts will not peel off – they will not show.

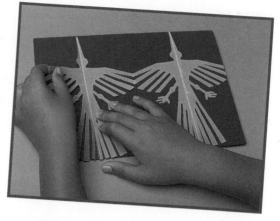

5 Score and fold a piece of A3 corrugated card in half widthways to make a card (see page 158).

6 Stick the condors on to the card with strong, clear glue.

FURTHER IDEAS
Invent your own fold-out Nazca style designs, using geometric shapes, straight lines and repeated patterns.

Fantasy Planets

Space ... the final frontier! What is out there? We know about the planets in our own solar system, but we cannot be sure about what lies beyond. Many people are fascinated by space and all the unanswered questions we have about the universe. With space, you can let your imagination run wild! In this project, spattering white paint on black card makes the perfect starry background for your own fantasy solar system. You can create all kinds of weird and wonderful planets using paint techniques and metallic pens.

1 Score and fold a large piece of black card in half. Dip the end of a toothbrush in some white paint and slowly run your finger over the bristles so the paint spatters onto the card. Allow to dry. You can spatter on a second colour if you like.

Note Practise spattering or sponging on scrap paper first, and always cover your work surface.

2 To make the planets, use compasses to draw four different sized circles on coloured card. Cut them out.

3

Put a circle on some newspaper. Dip a sponge in paint and lightly stroke the colour a little way across from one side. Stroking in a slight curve will make the planet look three-dimensional.

4

Sponge another colour across from the other side and then spatter more colours over the top with the toothbrush. Experiment with sponging, spattering and using metallic pens to decorate the other planets. Leave to dry.

5

Using the pattern on page 159 as a guide, draw a planet ring on card. Make sure it will fit over one of your planets. Then cut it out and lightly sponge some paint across it. Leave it to dry.

6

Slip the ring over a planet. Move the planets around on your space background until you are happy with the picture. Then stick them all in place with glue.

FURTHER IDEAS

Add aliens, rockets, meteors or space ships to your fantasy solar system.

Matisse Collage

Henri Matisse was a famous artist. He was influenced by many different styles. Once when Matisse was ill, he found it difficult to paint, so he made pictures by cutting shapes out of paper and sticking them down to make a collage. 'I am drawing directly in colour,' he said.

In this project I show you how to make a collage inspired by Matisse. There is a pattern on page 160 to help you, but if you feel confident, you could try cutting out your own picture freehand as Matisse did.

YOU WILL NEED

Thin card • Thick card
Compasses • Scissors
Empty ballpoint pen • Ruler
Glue stick • Pencil • Paper
Masking tape

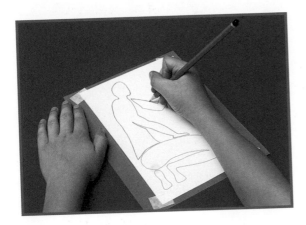

1 Transfer the pattern on page 160 on to thin card, or draw it freehand if you prefer.

2 On a different coloured piece of card, draw or transfer the plant design. Then, using compasses, draw a circle roughly 25mm (1in) across.

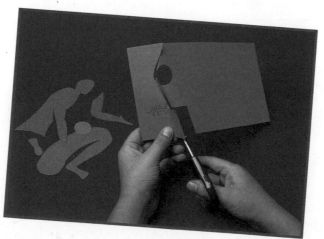

3 Cut out all of the shapes using scissors.

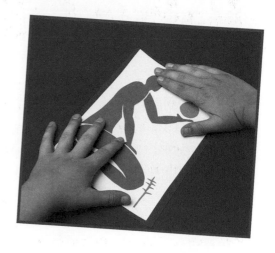

4

Take an A5 piece of thin card and trim 5–10mm (¼in) off each side. Try to leave an uneven edge as you cut.

5

Arrange the pieces on the card, leaving small gaps in the figure as shown. Glue them in place with a glue stick.

6

Score and fold a piece of A4 card in half and stick the finished collage on to the front.

FURTHER IDEAS

Cut out the shapes for figures, animals or plants, to make your own original collages.

It's a Goal!

Soccer is a brilliant game to play and to watch. Its history dates as far back as the ancient Chinese, Greek, Mayan and Egyptian societies. Modern football developed from games played in England in the nineteenth century. In 1863 these games were separated into rugby football, which is where American football comes from, and Association football, or soccer. You can make this soccer goal card by sewing the net with coloured thread, attaching the goal posts and finally putting the ball in the net – one-nil!

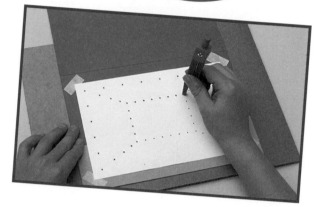

1 Score and fold a piece of thick A4 card in half. Stick a strip of green paper across the bottom.

2 Photocopy the dot pattern on page 159 and secure it to the front of the card with masking tape. Open the card and lay the front over a piece of thick corrugated cardboard to protect your work surface. Using the point of your compasses, pierce holes through the dots on the pattern. Then remove the pattern.

 Ask an adult to help you to photocopy the design.

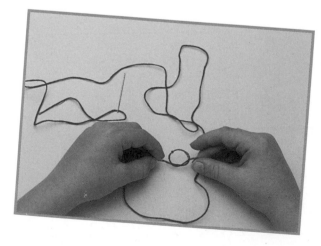

3 Thread one end of a long piece of coloured thread through the eye of a blunt-ended needle. Tie a large knot in the other end.

144

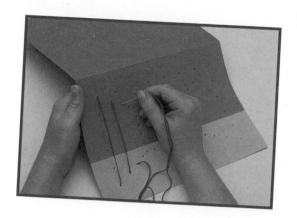

4

Push the needle up through the hole in the bottom left-hand corner and down through the hole in the top left-hand corner. Do the same for the next holes and continue until all the vertical lines are sewn.

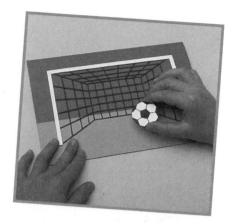

5

Now sew all the other lines of the net, as shown. You will use some holes more than once. If you run out of thread, tie a knot and thread your needle again.

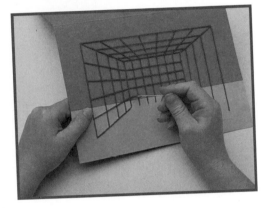

6

Transfer the goal posts and the football design on page 161 on to white card and cut them out. Colour the football with a black pen as shown. Use strong, clear glue to stick the goal posts and ball on to the card.

FURTHER IDEAS

Sew a basketball hoop, tennis racket, spider's web or even somebody's name to make an unusual card.

Spooky Wood

Woods can be very spooky at night. It is easy to imagine pairs of eyes peeping out from the dark. Woods and forests are often used to conjure up a spooky atmosphere in paintings, stories, poems and films. Collect interesting looking sticks and twigs to make the trees in this spooky wood card. Imagine the different creatures that live in the wood as you stick on their eyes. You could even write a spooky poem in the card.

YOU WILL NEED
Bright corrugated card • Thick card
Empty ballpoint pen • Ruler
Scissors • Plastic eyes
Masking tape • Pencil • Paper
Sticks • Strong, clear glue
Black felt

1 Enlarge the design on page 161 on a photocopier and transfer it on to the back of a piece of bright corrugated card. Enlarge the design by 141% to fit on to a sheet of A4, or by 200%, to fit on to a sheet of A3. Cut it out and score and fold along the dotted lines.

! Ask an adult to help you to photocopy the design.

2 Fold up the left-hand side of the corrugated card to make a rectangular tube. Squeeze a line of strong, clear glue on to the corrugated side of the end tab and stick it in place. Do the same on the right, but leave the top and bottom open.

3 Measure the flat area left in the middle. Cut out a piece of black felt the same size. Stick it on with strong, clear glue.

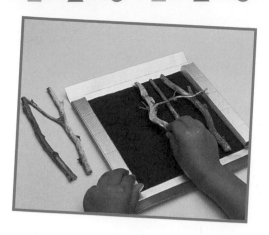

 Trim the sticks so they fit roughly inside the flat area. Then arrange them on top of the felt to look like a wood.

 Ask an adult to help you to cut the sticks.

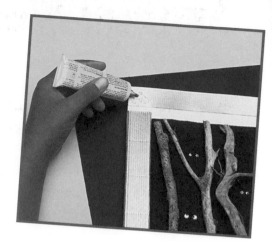

 When you are happy with the picture, glue down the sticks with strong, clear glue. Then stick pairs of plastic eyes in between the sticks. Leave to dry.

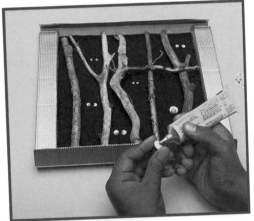

 Finish the frame by gluing the corners of the top and bottom flaps and sticking them down. Finally stick the finished frame on to a piece of folded card.

FURTHER IDEAS
Spray sticks with snow spray or silver paint and add a silvery moon to make a winter scene.

Funky Fish

Fish are very beautiful. It is amazing how many different shapes and colours there are. We have only explored one hundredth of the seabeds on our planet, so there may be even more weird and wonderful varieties of fish to be discovered in the future. In this project, fish are threaded on to metallic thread with beads, to make a bubbly underwater scene.

1 Score and fold a large piece of thick card in half. Using compasses and a pencil, draw a circle overlapping the fold and the bottom by about 5mm (¼in) as shown. Cut it out.

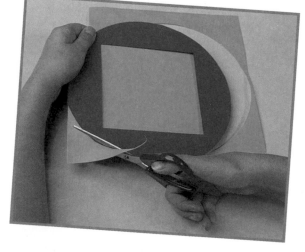

2 Open the circular card and draw a square on the front. Cut out the square to make a window. Stick a piece of coloured paper on the inside back of the card (the side you can see through the window) and trim to size.

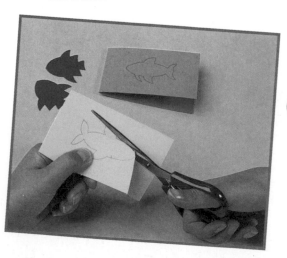

3 Fold three small pieces of thin coloured card in half. Transfer one of the fish designs on page 159 on to each piece of card. Cut out the fish – you will end up with two of each design.

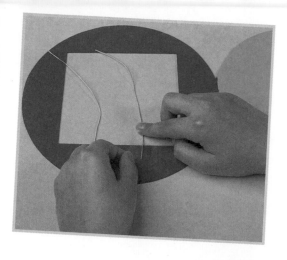

4 Lay two pieces of metallic thread over the window on the inside of the card. Secure them at the bottom with sticky tape.

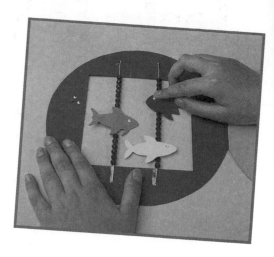

5 Thread some beads on to the first piece of metallic thread. Then take a pair of fish and put glue on one of them. Stick the fish together, sandwiching the thread between them as shown.

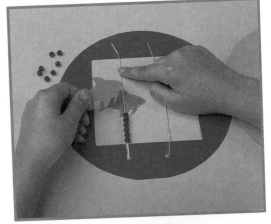

6 Thread on more beads and secure the top of the thread with sticky tape. Do the same on the other thread, using more beads and the other two fish. Finally stick plastic eyes on both sides of the fish using strong, clear glue.

FURTHER IDEAS
Make a card with a different shaped window. Add other sea creatures — an octopus, seahorse or dolphin.

Smiling Sunflower

Flowers are often used to cheer people up, and for special occasions like Mother's day and Valentine's day. Different flowers can mean different things. Red flowers are usually for love – roses, carnations and tulips. White flowers such as daisies and lilies represent innocence and purity. Pansies and poppies are for remembrance, sweet peas for goodbyes, and forget-me-nots speak for themselves! Sunflowers turn their heads to follow the sun across the sky. This one has a lovely smile and a stem made from flexible pipe cleaners, so that its head bobs cheerfully when it moves.

YOU WILL NEED
Card • Pipe cleaners
Scissors • Ruler • Pen
Plastic eyes • Pencil
Masking tape • Paper
Compasses • Eraser • Felt
Empty ballpoint pen
Strong, clear glue

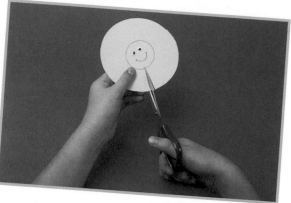

2 Cut a slit from the edge up to the small circle. Then cut a second slit next to it. Continue all of the way around the face. Carefully erase the pencil circle.

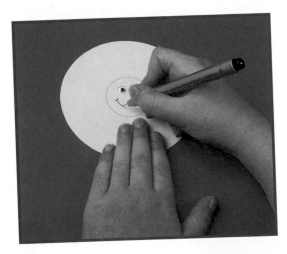

1 Use compasses and a pencil to draw a large circle on some yellow card, then cut it out. Draw a smaller circle in the middle for the sunflower's face. Stick on plastic eyes using strong, clear glue, and draw on a smile.

3 Fold every other petal away from you until there is a space between each one. Then hold all the folded petals together and wrap the end of a pipe cleaner round them until they are secure. The rest of this pipe cleaner will be the sunflower's stem.

Twist more pipe cleaners around the stem to make it longer and thicker. Cut two sets of leaves out of felt. Push the leaves between the pipe cleaners as shown.

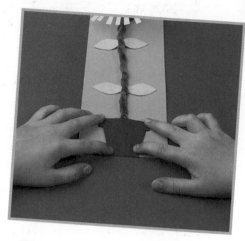

5

Transfer the pattern for the flower pot on page 159 on to card. Cut it out. Score along the dotted lines as shown and fold back the tabs.

6

Score and fold a piece of A4 size card in half lengthways. Glue the bottom half of the flower stem to the card. Put glue on the flower pot tabs and stick the pot over the stem.

FURTHER IDEAS
Create flowers using textured papers or metallic card. Try making several layers of petals.

Pop-up Dinosaur

Millions of years ago there were no people, and dinosaurs ruled the earth. We know from digging up their bones what kinds of dinosaurs existed, their sizes and shapes and even what they ate. But we do not know what colours they were. So when you make this pop-up dinosaur card, imagine the colours for yourself and create a prehistoric world of your own. There are patterns for the Tyrannosaurus Rex and the Pteranodon in the back of the book, but you could draw any of your favourite dinosaurs – or even invent your own.

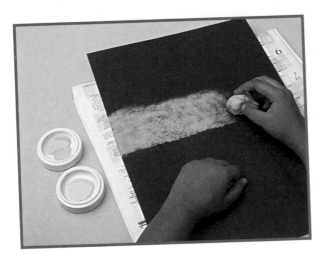

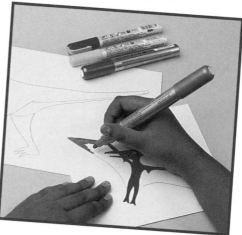

 Transfer the Tyrannosaurus Rex and Pteranodon designs on page 160 on to thick card. Colour them in using paint pens.

YOU WILL NEED

Thick card • Scissors
Coloured and metallic paint pens
Strong, clear glue • Pencil
Ruler • Masking tape • Paper
Thin black pen • Acrylic paint
Natural sponge

 Score and fold a large piece of thick card in half. On the top half of the inside, sponge on a strip of paint to suggest a landscape. Leave to dry.

Note Sponging two similar colours on top of each other can make a landscape look more realistic.

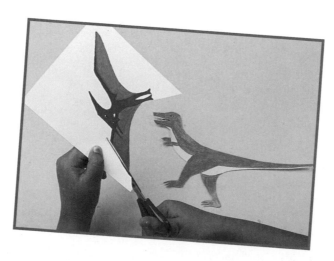

 Draw the outlines and the eyes with a thin black pen. Carefully cut the dinosaurs out. If some areas are difficult to cut out, colour them black so that they will not show up.

152

Decide where you want your dinosaur to stand, and mark the spot lightly with a pencil. Fold the card inside out. From the fold side, cut two slits up to the mark you have made.

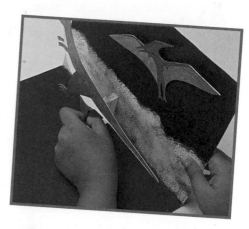

Open up the card and press between the cuts to push out a tab. Then close the card again with the tab pushed out and press. This will help to fold the tab in the right position.

Open the card and stick the Tyrannosaurus's leg on to the tab with strong, clear glue. Glue the Pteranodon on to the background.

Note To make the Pteranodon stand out from the card, stick a little pad of folded card on the back before gluing it in place.

FURTHER IDEAS

Make pop-up scenery for your dinosaur world: hills, trees, plants, mountains — even a volcano!

Jazzy Guitar

Guitars are played all over the world to make all kinds of music – from Spanish flamenco and folk music to pop, rock and jazz. They usually have six strings, although there are twelve-string guitars as well. The strings play a different note depending on how taut they are. They can be adjusted to the right pitch using a special tuning key. You can make a card in the shape of a guitar and add strings made from coloured thread.

YOU WILL NEED

Card • Scissors
Glue stick • Pencil • Paper
Masking tape • Compasses
Coloured thread • Blunt-ended needle
Thick corrugated cardboard
Paint pens

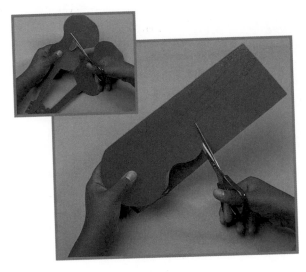

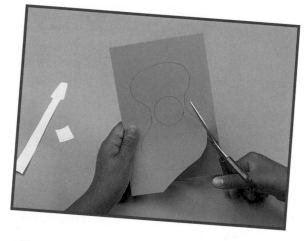

 Transfer the inner guitar pattern and the neck and soundboard patterns on to coloured card and cut them out.

 Score and fold a piece of thick coloured card in half and transfer the outer guitar design on page 159 on to it. Make sure that the dotted edges marked on the pattern go over the fold line. Cut out the guitar. Open the card and cut out the circle in the middle from the front of the card only.

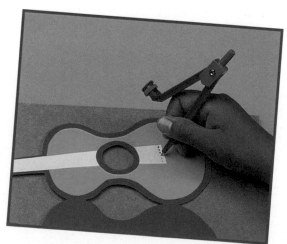

 Stick the inner guitar, neck and soundboard on to the card. Open up the card, then place it over some thick corrugated cardboard. Pierce the sets of holes on the neck and the soundboard with compasses.

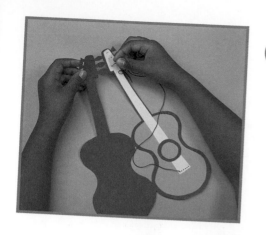

4 Thread one end of a piece of coloured thread through the eye of a blunt-ended needle and tie a knot in the other end. Sew up through the far left hole at the bottom and down through the far left hole at the top.

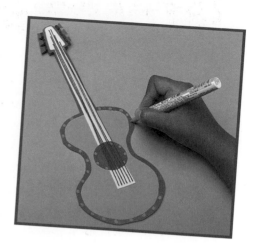

5 Gently pull the thread through until taut. Do not pull it too tight, or the card will bend. Then wrap the end round the bottom left tuning key and tie a knot. Repeat for the other five strings.

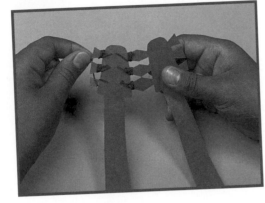

6 Decorate your guitar by drawing big dots around the edge with a paint pen.

Note If you find knotting the thread difficult, you can tape the loose ends at the back.

FURTHER IDEAS
Try making other musical instruments. A banjo has five strings, a double bass has four and a harp has lots and lots.

Winter Window

Many cultures around the world have a winter festival. Most of them are linked to the winter solstice. This is the time of the shortest day and the longest night of the year. Some of the festivals celebrated during winter are Christmas, Bodhi Day, Hanukkah and Yule. Winter is a lovely time to gather with family and friends and stay warm by the fire. You can make a winter window card using polystyrene balls for snow and a clear plastic bag such as a sandwich or freezer bag for the window.

YOU WILL NEED
Thick card • High-density foam
Ruler • Pencil • Sticky tape
Strong, clear glue • Glue stick
Masking tape • Paper
Small polystyrene balls
Sandwich bag
Scissors

 1

Cut out two pieces of card, one 42cm x 21cm (16½in x 8¼in), and one 21cm (8¼in) square. Fold the big one in half.

 2 On the inside front of the folded card, measure 4cm (1½in) in from each side and draw lines to make a square. Cut out the square.

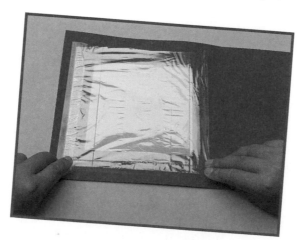

 3

Open up the card again and lay a clear sandwich bag over the square. You may need to trim the top of the bag to fit. Use sticky tape to stick it on at the bottom and sides. Do not stretch the bag too tightly, as this will warp the card.

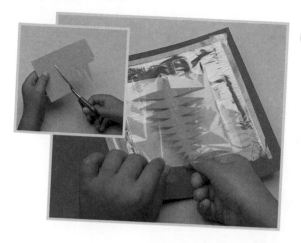

4

Draw a tree on high-density foam and cut it out. Put a line of glue down the middle of the tree and stick it inside the bag. Make sure the glued side of the tree is uppermost.

5

Sprinkle some polystyrene balls in to the bag and tape up the top.

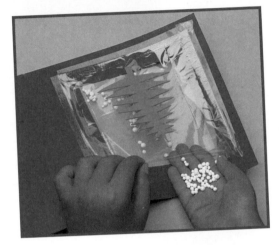

6

Spread strong, clear glue on the inside of the card window frame. Stick the square piece of card on top.

FURTHER IDEAS
You can make all sorts of things to stand in your snow storm – try a snowman, a house, a reindeer or a penguin.

Techniques

Ask an adult to help you to photocopy the patterns.

Transferring a design

You can photocopy the patterns on pages 159–161 and transfer them on to card using the technique shown below. Use the photocopier to enlarge or reduce the designs if you need to.

 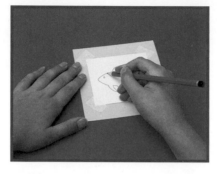 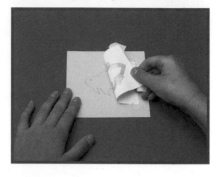

1 Photocopy the design. Turn over the photocopy and scribble over the lines with a soft pencil.

2 Turn the photocopy over and tape it to your card using masking tape. Then go over the lines of the design with a pencil.

3 Peel back the photocopy to reveal the transferred design.

Scoring and folding card

Dotted lines on the patterns need to be scored and folded. You can also use scoring to help make neat cards. Find the centre line by measuring the halfway point and score and fold as shown below.

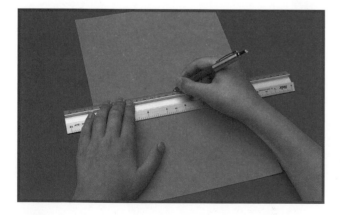 

1 Score a line across the middle of the card with a ballpoint pen that has run out of ink.

2 Fold the card and run the back of your fingernail along the fold to press it down. If the edges are not exactly square, you can trim them with scissors.

Patterns

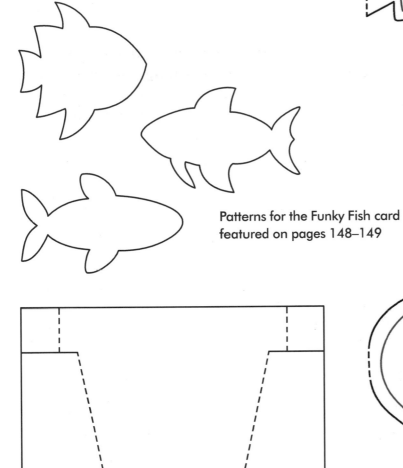

Patterns for the Funky Fish card featured on pages 148–149

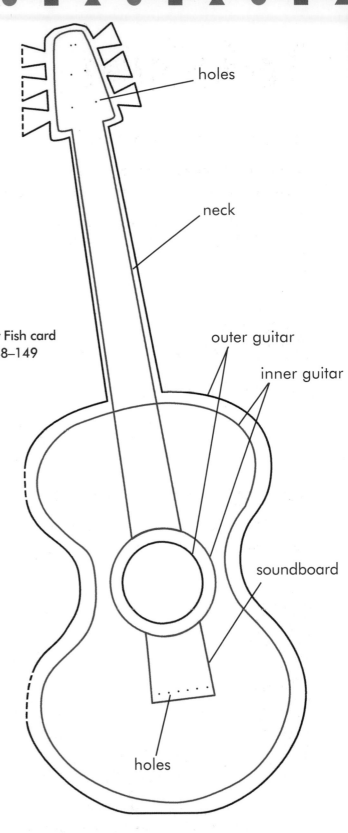

holes

neck

outer guitar

inner guitar

soundboard

holes

Pattern for the flower pot in the Smiling Sunflower card featured on pages 150–151

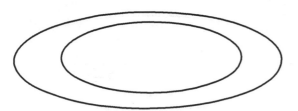

Pattern for the planet ring used in the Fantasy Planets card featured on pages 140–141

Pattern for the Jazzy Guitar card featured on pages 154–155

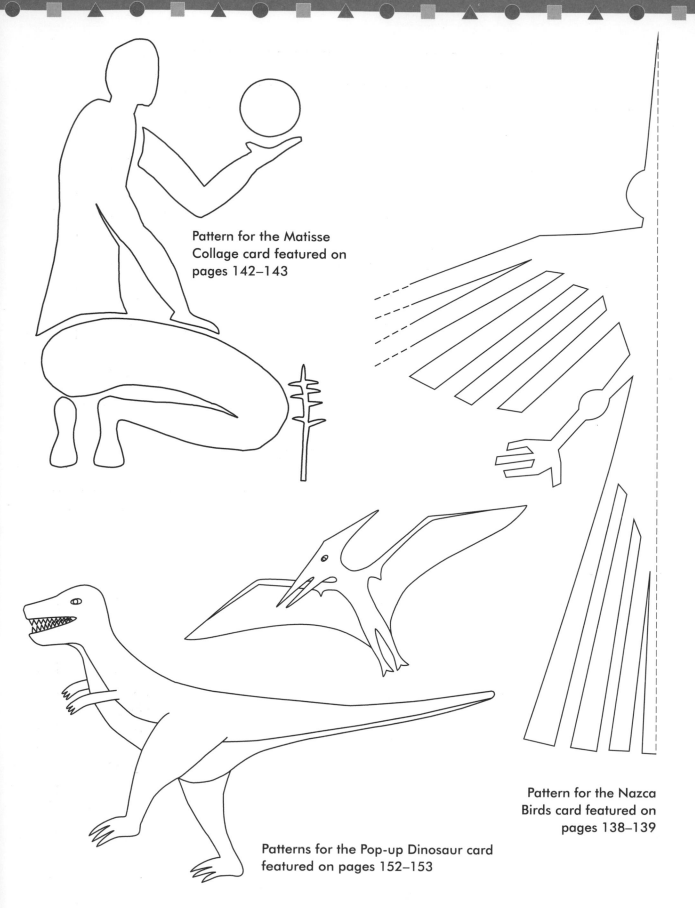

Pattern for the Matisse
Collage card featured on
pages 142–143

Pattern for the Nazca
Birds card featured on
pages 138–139

Patterns for the Pop-up Dinosaur card
featured on pages 152–153

Pattern for the frame of the Spooky
Wood card featured on pages 146–147

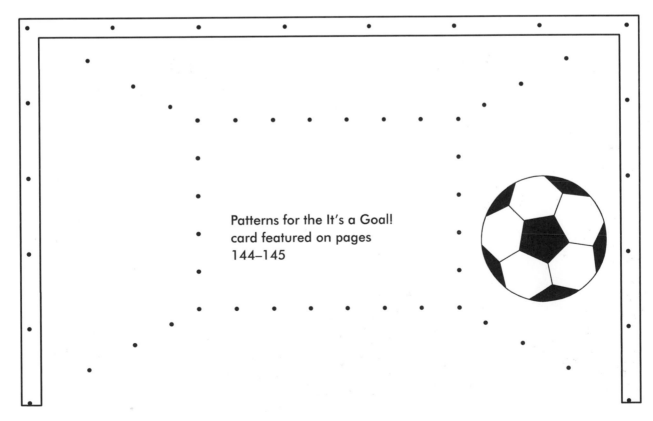

Patterns for the It's a Goal!
card featured on pages
144–145

Collage

by Judy Balchin

You have probably been creating collages for years without even knowing it. The word 'collage' comes from the French word meaning 'to stick' and we can all remember creating pictures by sticking paper shapes on to a piece of card.

Over the years, many artists have used collage in their work. Matisse was a very famous French artist. As he got older, he found painting quite difficult, so he started tearing and cutting up pieces of coloured paper to make his pictures.

Beautiful collages were created by a lady called Mary Delaney who lived in the eighteenth century. She was an expert needlewoman and made delicate collages using plant life as her theme. She did not start making her collages until she was seventy-two – a craft for all ages!

You may think that only paper is used in collage, but that is far from the truth. Twentieth century artist, Georges Braque, used very unusual materials in his work. He introduced imitation wood paper and fabric to his pictures. Perhaps some of the most unusual collages come from an artist called Kurt Schwitters, who made pictures using rubbish that he found in his city life, such as tickets, rags, advertisements and newspaper.

You don't have to be particularly artistic to create a collage. It really is a question of colour and balance. Pieces can be moved round and played with until you are satisfied with the arrangement, and then simply stuck down.

If, like me, you are a hoarder, then this section is definitely for you. I've always been drawn to brightly coloured pieces of fabric, coloured papers, ribbons, sequins and jewels. I must admit to having boxes of bits hidden here and there around my home. This section has given me the excuse to get all those boxes out. Felt, foil, feathers and foam; leaves, seeds and even plastic and polythene can be used for collage. The list is endless. A walk along a beach or in the countryside can provide you with a wealth of material to use. Alternatively just look around your own home and see what you can come up with.

So there you sit with your boxes of goodies. Perhaps the next question is what to make a picture of. As you work through this section, you will come across collages of butterflies, fish, aliens, spiders, flowers, fairies and even an Egyptian god. By the time you have completed all the projects in this section, you will have created a collage art gallery. Perhaps, more importantly, it will have inspired you to create your own collages using your interests, hobbies or even your favourite colour as a theme. Good luck with your sticking!

Sea Scene

A third of the surface of the world is covered by water. These seas and oceans are full of life. Most fish live in the upper part of the seas, down to a depth of 600m (2000 feet). Below this lurk strange deep-sea fish living in the darker waters. In this project we create the movement of water using layered and scrunched tissue paper. Our brightly coloured fish dives across the collage, its jewelled decorations catching the light.

YOU WILL NEED

A4 piece of thick card
Thin white card
Coloured tissue paper
Watered down PVA glue
Paste brushes
Scissors
Pencil
Coloured gems

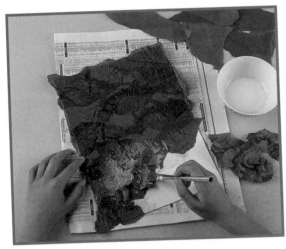

1 Paste a section of your base board generously with some watered down PVA glue. Lay a piece of scrunched up tissue paper on to the glue and dab it with a paste brush until it lies flat, but with scrunched creases, as shown. Overlap the next piece of tissue paper slightly and continue in this way until the board is covered.

2 When the board is dry, use scissors to cut off the overhanging tissue paper.

3

Transfer the fish pattern on page 187 on to thin white card. Page 184 shows you how to transfer a pattern. Cut the fish shape out. Scrunch and glue pieces of tissue paper in a lighter colour over the surface of the card fish.

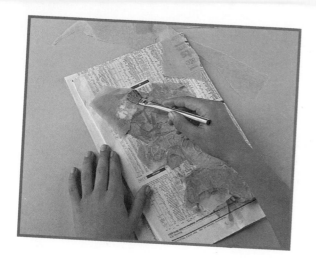

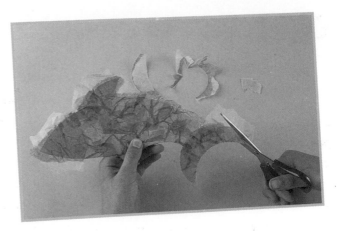

 Use a different coloured tissue paper to cover the head, tails and fins. Scrunch and glue as before.

5 Tear circles of tissue paper and stick them on to the body section. Leave to dry. Cut off the overhanging tissue paper.

6

Glue the fish to the base board. Glue one coloured gem to each spot on the fish's body. Glue a gem in place for the fish's eye. You can glue a smaller gem on top to make a realistic pupil for the eye.

FURTHER IDEAS
Make a fish bowl filled with smaller fish made in the same way.

Butterflies

The beautiful colours of the butterfly inspired this collage.
There are about one million known kinds of insect. A lot of
them use their shape and colour either to attract a mate or to
scare off an enemy. How many brightly coloured insects can
you think of? Multicoloured sequins are the perfect decoration
for our butterfly collage. The wings shimmer against the dark
background, giving a real feeling of movement.

YOU WILL NEED
Dark-coloured thick card, 8
x 24cm (3 x 9½in)
Thin card for template
Thin coloured card
Coloured pipe cleaners
Coloured sequins
Pencil
Scissors
PVA glue

1 Make a template of the butterfly pattern
on page 186. Page 184 shows you how
to make a template. Draw round the
template three times on thin coloured
card. Cut out three butterflies.

2 To make the butterfly bodies and
antennae, cut an 18cm (7in) length of
coloured pipe cleaner for each butterfly.
Bend them in half and curl the ends as
shown. Glue one body down the centre
of each butterfly.

3

Glue coloured sequins on to
the card wings, overlapping
them slightly so that the card
is completely covered.

 Bend the wings upwards slightly either side of the body.

5 Turn the butterflies over and run one line of glue down each body section.

Press the butterflies on to your dark-coloured thick card so that they overhang the edges of the card.

FURTHER IDEAS

Create a shimmering dragonfly using shiny fabric for the wings and beads and gems for the body.

Roman Mosaic

The Romans loved to decorate their large city villas. Though they were often quite plain on the outside, inside could be sumptuous. They used small pieces of coloured stone, called 'tesserae', to cover their floors, placing them so that they formed intricate patterns. These were called mosaics. This project shows you how to make a mosaic starfish collage using small pieces of coloured foam. Don 't worry if all the pieces are not exactly square – your collage will look more realistic if they are slightly irregular.

YOU WILL NEED
20cm² (8in²) square of thick black card
Three sheets of coloured foam
Thin card • Scissors
PVA glue • Pencil
Ruler

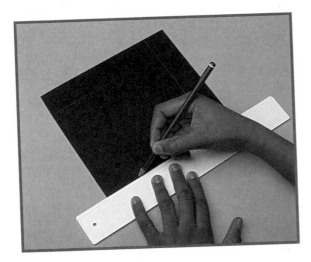

 Use a pencil and ruler to draw a line 33mm (1¼in) from each edge of your thick card, to create a border.

2 Cut 1.5cm (½in) strips from two pieces of different coloured foam. Mark 1.5cm (½in) sections all along the strips, and cut them into squares.

Glue a row of foam squares around the edge of the black card, using alternating colours. Glue a second row of squares inside the first row as shown.

4 Photocopy the starfish design on page 185 on to thin card and cut it out to make a template. Place the starfish template on a coloured piece of foam and draw round it with a pencil. Cut it out.

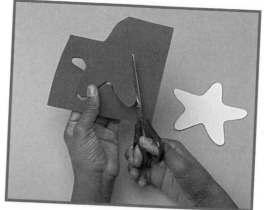

Ask an adult to help you use the photocopier.

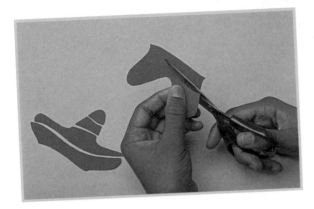

5 Draw wavy lines across the starfish with a pencil. Cut along the wavy lines. Arrange the cut pieces into a starfish again in the middle of your mosaic border.

6 Glue the pieces down.

FURTHER IDEAS
Make a dolphin picture in a mosaic frame.

Creepy Crawlies

Some people are frightened of spiders, so this project could be a bit of a challenge! They are, however, fascinating creatures. Did you know that most spiders have eight eyes and that they taste through their feet? Some large spiders can live to twenty-five years and some South American varieties actually eat birds! What other amazing facts can you find out about spiders? These colourful pompom spiders with their pipe cleaner legs and wobbly eyes aren't quite so scary, so have fun creating this creepy crawly collage.

YOU WILL NEED
Thick card, 30 x 25cm
(11¾ x 10in)
Textured wallpaper
Coloured pompoms
Coloured pipe cleaners
Coloured wool • Plastic eyes
Scissors • PVA glue
Sticky tape

1 Cut out irregular paper stone shapes from wallpaper. Arrange them on your thick card base board to look like a stone wall. Some of the end 'stones' will have to be cut in half to fit. Glue them on to the base card and leave to dry.

2 Turn the base board over and tape a length of wool to the top right-hand corner. Wrap the wool round the card to create a fan-shaped web on the front. Tape the end of the wool to the back of the card to secure it.

3 Wrap another length of wool across the bottom of the card in the same way, and tape the end at the back to secure it.

 4

Cut two pipe cleaners in half. Tie the four pieces together in the middle with a piece of wool to make the legs of the spider.

 5

Bend the legs as shown. Glue a pompom body to the place where the legs meet. Glue two plastic eyes on to the pompom. Make three spiders in the same way.

 6

Glue two spiders on to the stone wall and one in the centre of the web.

FURTHER IDEAS
Make centipedes from pompoms with snipped felt strips for legs, glued on to a background of paper leaves.

Sunflower Card

This project uses real sunflower seeds to decorate the centre of a paper sunflower. Sunflower seeds, and the seeds of other plants such as the poppy, are edible (unless you are allergic to nuts and seeds!) We grind seeds to spice our food, add them to our breads and cook with them. Oil can be extracted from certain seeds and, of course, seeds are also planted to grow a new crop. Try writing a list of different seeds and what we can do with them.

YOU WILL NEED
Coloured thick card
23 x 46cm (9 x 18in)
Lighter-coloured thin card
21cm (8¼in) square
Coloured crepe paper
Sunflower seeds
Scissors • Ruler
PVA glue • Paste spreader
Pencil • Compasses

 Score and fold the rectangle of thick card down the middle to make a greetings card (see page 184). Glue the square of lighter-coloured card to the middle of the front.

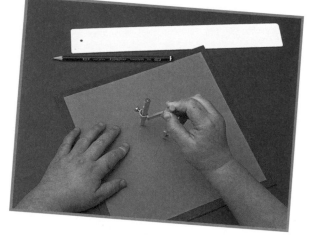

 Find the centre of the square card by drawing in the diagonals with a pencil and ruler. Set your compasses to 3.5cm (1¼in) from the point to the pencil. Put the point in the centre of the square and draw a circle.

 Take two 7 x 50cm (2¾ x 19¾in) strips of coloured crepe paper. Cut petal shapes along one long edge using the pattern on page 186 to help you.

 Run a 1cm (½in) line of glue around the outside of the pencil circle. Press the straight edge of the petal strip round the circle, scrunching the paper to make it fit. Complete one circle.

 Run another line of glue round the inside of the circle and press the second petal strip round it in the same way.

 Spread the circle generously with glue, overlapping the base of the petals slightly. Press the sunflower seeds into the glue and leave to dry.

FURTHER IDEAS
Make a bright poppy in the same way, using poppy seeds for the flower centre.

Fairy Card

Every country has its own stories about mythical creatures. Fairies, elves, gnomes, goblins, pixies, leprechauns – how many different creatures can you come up with? Fairy tales have entertained children throughout the world for hundreds of years. These stories are often exciting, sometimes scary and frequently offer a moral at the end of the tale. This project uses shimmering fabric, glittery cord and sparkly gems and beads to create a magical fairy card.

YOU WILL NEED
Coloured card, 18 x 21cm
(7 x 8¼in)
Coloured felt
Shiny fabric • Silver cord
Small gems • Star sequins
Large glittery beads
PVA glue • Scissors
Pencil

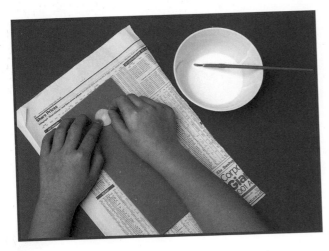

1 Score and fold the coloured card lengthways to make a greetings card (see page 184). Transfer the face pattern on page 185 on to felt (also see page 184). Cut it out and glue it to the front of the card.

2 Glue two small gems to the face for eyes. Squeeze a blob of glue on to the top of the circle. Crumple some silver cord and press it into the glue to make hair.

3 Make wing templates using the pattern on page 185. Draw round them on shiny fabric and cut them out. Squeeze some glue just below the head and press the ends of the wings into place.

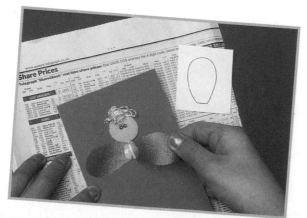

 4

Cut a 12cm (4¾in) length of silver cord. Thread each end with a bead and knot to secure. Place the piece of cord across the wings and glue it in the middle. This will make the fairy's arms.

5

Cut a 30cm (11¾in) length of silver cord for the legs. Thread each end with a bead and knot as before. Fold the cord in half and glue the fold just under the arms.

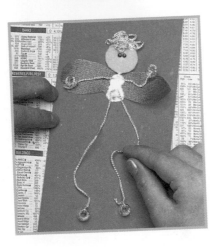

6

Use the pattern on page 185 to make a template of the dress shape, cut it out from felt and stick it onto the card just below the head. Glue a halo of star-shaped sequins around your fairy's head, and one sequin to the dress.

FURTHER IDEAS

Why not make a pixie to go with your fairy card? Put a feather in his cap.

Junk Truck

Everything in nature is recycled. Vegetation and animal remains feed the soil, which in its turn, nourishes new life. We can play our part by recycling rubbish that is not biodegradable, that is, it doesn't rot away. Nowadays there are factories that recycle paper, glass, aluminium cans, car tyres, some plastics, old clothes and lots more. You can create a collage using junk found around your home. Collect plastic, polythene and polystyrene packaging instead of putting it in the bin. Look for paper, string and bottle tops too – you will be amazed at how much junk you find.

YOU WILL NEED
Cardboard box lid
Junk: coloured plastic containers,
lids, polythene, string, polystyrene,
foam packing
and plastic netting
Kitchen foil
Permanent felt tip pen
PVA glue • Scissors

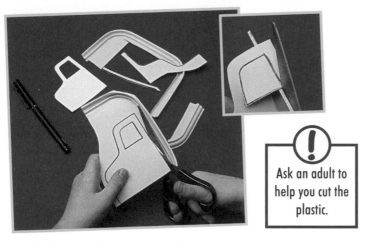

(!) Ask an adult to help you cut the plastic.

1 Make templates from the pattern on page 186, using the technique shown on page 184. Place the cab template on a piece of coloured plastic and draw round it with a permanent felt tip pen. Cut it out.

2 Cut a piece of coloured polythene slightly larger than the window hole. Glue it on to the back of the plastic so that it covers the hole.

Note To cut the window hole, first cut across the upright bar at the back of the cab. This makes it easier to move the scissors, and will not show when you stick the cab down.

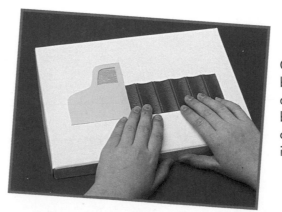

3 Glue the cab on to the box lid. Use a template as before to cut the back of the truck out of coloured plastic. Glue it behind the cab.

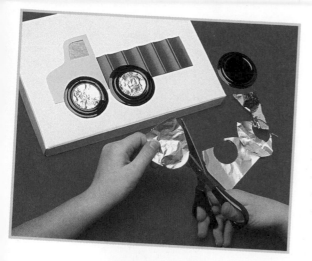

Cut three circles of black plastic for the wheels. Cut three smaller circles of foil and glue one to the middle of each wheel. Glue the wheels along the bottom of the truck.

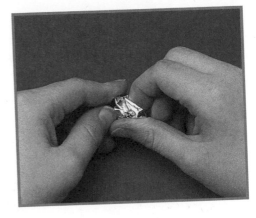

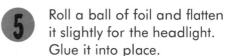
Roll a ball of foil and flatten it slightly for the headlight. Glue it into place.

Now fill your truck with junk! Cut your bits of junk into small pieces and glue them to the back of the truck.

FURTHER IDEAS
Make a junk robot from the plastic tray inside a box of chocolates.

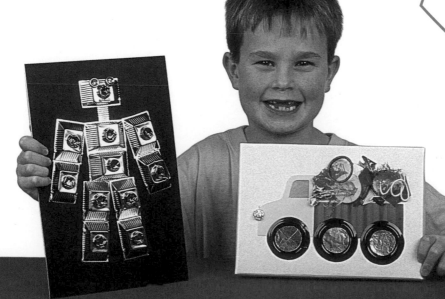

Egyptian God

The Ancient Egyptians believed in many gods. Some of the gods shown in their pictures looked half animal and half human. Anubis had the head of a jackal – a dog-like animal. The Egyptians believed that he was in charge of the underworld. Priests who prepared bodies for burial wore Anubis masks while performing their duties. In this collage, Anubis is shown wearing a sparkling headdress, and standing in front of some sandpaper pyramids.

YOU WILL NEED
Thick coloured card 25 x 23cm (10 x 9in)
Thin card • Black felt
Sheet of sandpaper
Gold sequin trim
Coloured gem
Scissors • Old scissors
PVA glue • Ruler
Chalk • Pencil

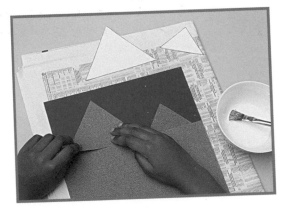

1 Glue a 15 x 23cm (6 x 9in) piece of sandpaper across the lower half of a 25 x 23cm (10 x 9in) piece of thick coloured card. Make pyramid templates as shown on page 184, using the patterns on page 187, and draw round them on the back of another piece of sandpaper. Cut out the pyramid shapes and glue them on the horizon line.

2 Make templates of the Anubis patterns. Lay them on black felt back to front, and draw round them with a piece of chalk. Cut out the felt shapes, cutting along the inside of the chalk lines.

(!) Ask an adult to help you cut the sandpaper, and always use old scissors.

3 Spread the felt pieces with glue and then turn them over and stick them on to the sandpaper background.

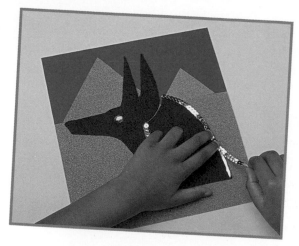

 4
Glue a coloured gem in place for the eye. Squeeze a line of glue down the left-hand and right-hand edges of the headdress shape. Press a length of sequin trim on to the glue.

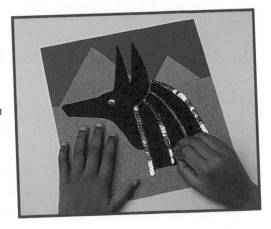

 5
Use chalk to draw two curved lines between the sequined edges of the headdress. Squeeze glue down each line and glue lengths of sequin trim in place.

 6
Trim the ends as shown. Glue a length of sequin trim along the top and bottom of the headdress. Leave to dry.

FURTHER IDEAS
Make a Chinese dragon using felt and fabric. What other animals can you think of that are connected to certain countries?

Leaf Card

Leaves and plants are very important to our planet. They take in carbon dioxide from the air and give off oxygen which we need to survive. Dried leaves and fruits provide us with beautiful shapes and textures which are ideal for collage work. Just look at the delicate skeleton leaf. You can see clearly the fine network of strands that kept the leaf supplied with water and nutrients. Use an earthy coloured card for this project, as it will really set off these natural forms.

YOU WILL NEED

Thin coloured card
Coloured handmade paper
Skeleton leaf
Dried orange slice • Raffia
PVA glue • Glue spreader
Pencil • Scissors

1 Cut an 18 x 9.5cm (7 x 3¾in) rectangle of thin coloured card. Score and fold it down the middle, as shown on page 184. Measure and cut a 9 x 9.5cm (3½ x 3¾in) rectangle of handmade paper.

2 Tear a small strip from each edge of the handmade paper, to give it a rough-edged look. Glue the rectangle to the front of your card.

3 Put the skeleton leaf on a piece of scrap paper and spread it carefully with a little glue. Press it gently on to the front of your card and leave to dry.

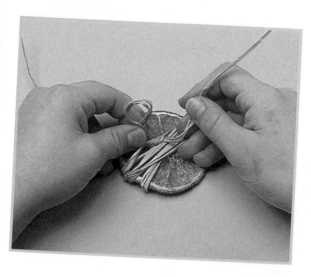

 4

Wrap a dried orange slice with raffia and tie it in a bow at the front. Trim the ends of the raffia using scissors.

 5 Glue the wrapped orange slice to the card at the base of the leaf.

6

Cut two 2.5cm (1in) squares of coloured card and glue them to your leaf card: one to the top right and one to the bottom left.

FURTHER IDEAS

Make a tree with a raffia trunk, paper leaves and card and mustard seed oranges. Add grass made from dried herbs sprinkled over wet glue.

Alien

The Earth is a small planet in a huge universe. The universe is made up of countless planets and stars. Nobody knows how big the universe is or if it has any limits. Do you think there is life on other planets? If you think there is, what do you think these alien life forms would look like? In this project, metal foil is used to create the alien. Backed with colourful planets drifting in a dark sky, this collage is definitely out of this world!

 1 Draw round a plate and cup to make a circle and a semicircle on a piece of thin white card. Cut out the shapes. Glue torn pieces of tissue paper over the card shapes and leave to dry.

2 Cut off the overhanging tissue paper. Glue the large semicircle to the bottom of a 20 x 30cm (8 x 11¾in) piece of coloured card. Glue the smaller circle to the top right-hand corner.

Ask an adult to help you use the photocopier.

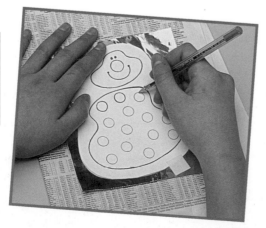

3 Photocopy the alien pattern on page 185 on to paper. Cut round the pattern, leaving space around the edges as shown. Place a piece of embossing foil slightly larger than the pattern on a folded newspaper. Lay the pattern on top and tape it to the foil. Use a ballpoint pen to trace the design through on to the foil. Press firmly.

Remove the pattern and cut out the alien head and body from the foil. Turn them over. Glue them on to the planet card.

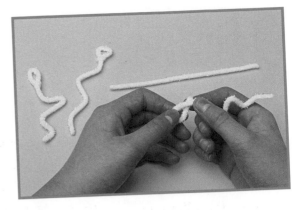

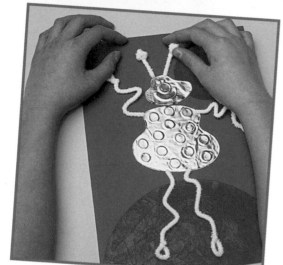

5 Bend four pipe cleaners into zigzags. Bend one end of each pipe cleaner into a circle to make hands and feet. Twist to secure.

Glue the pipe cleaner arms and legs into position. Cut two 10cm (4in) lengths of pipe cleaner to make antennae. Roll one end of each length into a ball. Glue the antennae on to the top of the alien's head. Decorate with sequins.

FURTHER IDEAS
Make a rocket collage using silver card, hologram card and sequins. Use decorative floss for the rocket's fiery trail.

Techniques

Making a greetings card

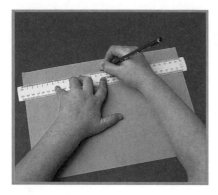

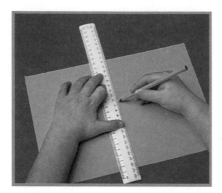

1 Measure halfway across your card and mark the halfway points at the top and bottom.

2 Using a ballpoint pen that has run out of ink, and a ruler, score a line down the card between the marks.

3 Fold the card along the scored line to make a nice sharp crease.

(!) Ask an adult to help you to photocopy the patterns.

Transferring a pattern

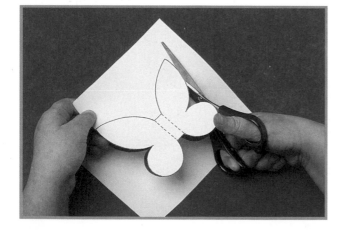

1 Photocopy the pattern on to thin white card. You can enlarge it on the photocopier if you need to. You can use the photocopy for your project, or you can cut out the pattern to make a template.

2 Draw round your template to make the shapes you need for your collage projects.

Patterns

Pattern for the Roman Mosaic featured on pages 168–169

Pattern for the Alien collage featured on pages 182–183

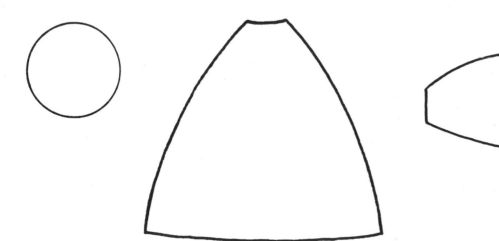

Patterns for the face, dress and wings for the Fairy Card featured on pages 174–175

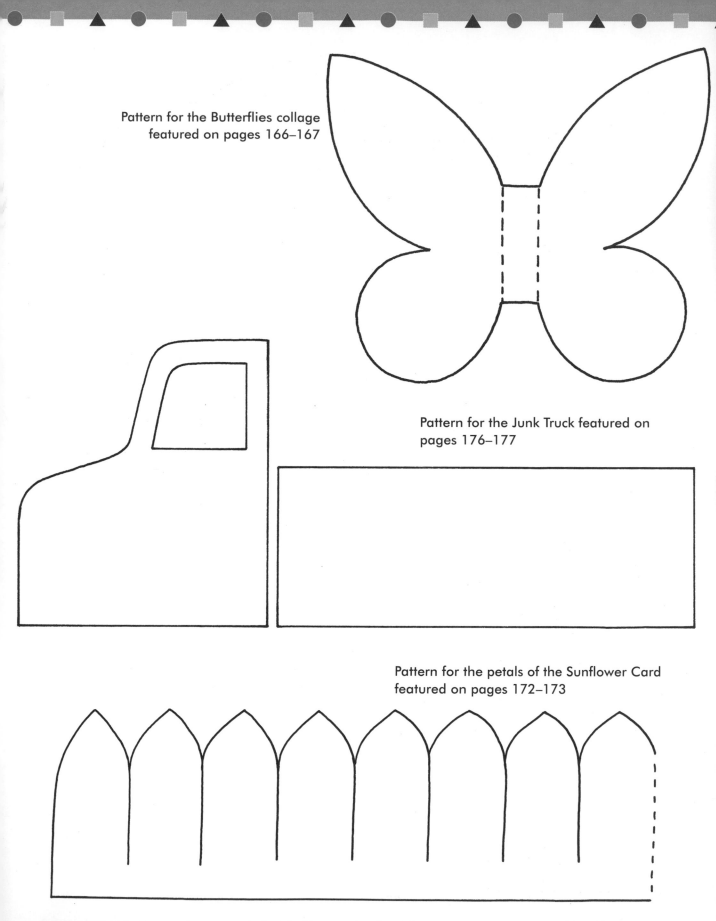

Pattern for the Butterflies collage featured on pages 166–167

Pattern for the Junk Truck featured on pages 176–177

Pattern for the petals of the Sunflower Card featured on pages 172–173

The fish pattern for the Sea Scene
featured on pages 164–165

Pattern for the Egyptian God and pyramids
featured on pages 178–179

Clay Modelling

by Greta Speechley

People have been modelling clay for thousands of years, and pottery fragments have been found that date back as far as 1200 BC. These early pots were baked in bonfires and, because the heat was not very intense, they were very fragile. As a result, only broken pieces of some of the vessels have survived to the present day. Some pots and models have been discovered in tombs and burial places, and you can see wonderful collections of these in many museums. Lots of these ancient vessels were highly decorated with painted figures and animals, which tell wonderful stories of how life used to be. The methods used by craftspeople in those far-off days were simple. Items were hand-modelled and moulded into useful and decorative shapes, just like they are today.

I have taken my inspiration from nature, the world around us, and the simple techniques used by our ancestors to show how easy it is to create colourful and fun models, zany pots, crazy containers and painted tiles. Each project shows a different way of using clay and suggests how you can paint your finished pieces with poster or acrylic paints. You might want to copy each one exactly to start off with, but I am sure that once you have done this, you will want to create your own unique pot or model.

It is a good idea to start using a sketch book or to keep a scrap book so that you can keep a note of the colours you like and use them on your models. Cut out bits of fabric, or snippets from magazines. Think about texture – do you want a smooth finish, or would you prefer a rough surface? Look at pottery and sculpture from different countries and decide which you prefer. My favourite pieces come from Mexico and South America. I love the little figures and curious animals that cover these pots, and they are always painted in such lovely vibrant colours.

I have used air-drying clay for all the projects in this section. It is easy to use and is available from most craft shops. There are quite a few different types. Try to find one that is squidgy when you poke it, rather than being hard. Clay is wonderful to work with – if it does not look quite right, you can just squash it up and start all over again, and it can be used to make almost anything. I am sure you will come up with lots of ideas of your own and have great fun clay modelling. The only limit is your imagination. Have fun!

Note If you have access to a kiln, you can use real clay for all the projects except the solid swinging tiger on pages 198–199. You must ask an adult to use the kiln for you.

Techniques

Clay is really easy to work with. You can model straight from a ball of clay, you can coil up long thin sausages, or you can make flat slabs which can be used to build boxes and containers. Practise these techniques before you start the projects.

Pinching out shapes

This very simple modelling technique is great for making small pots and bowls, and for modelling animals. Hold a small ball of clay in one hand and press your thumb into the clay to make a hole.

Gently squeeze the clay between your thumb and fingers and work evenly round the ball of clay to open up the shape. Stop from time to time to see how your shape is progressing.

Note Before you start working on a project, always soften the clay by kneading it in your hands.

Rolling coils

You can use long clay sausages (coils) to build pots of any size and shape. The coils are made by rolling out the clay with your hands. For small pots, coils need to be about the thickness of your finger – make them a bit thicker for larger pots.

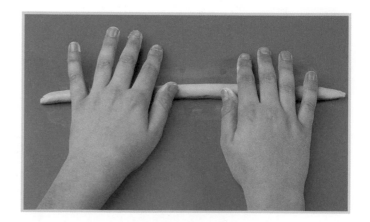

Making slabs

Flat slabs of clay can be used for tiles or for building boxes and containers. You will need a piece of cotton cloth (old cotton sheeting is ideal), a rolling pin and two lengths of wood. Place a ball of clay between the wooden lengths and flatten it with the rolling pin. The thickness of the wood controls the thickness of the slab.

Note It is much easier to roll out several small slabs than to try and roll out one huge one.

Cutting out shapes

Use a paper pattern and a knife to cut out your design. Leave the clay to harden slightly before moving it, otherwise you may distort the shape.

You can use pastry cutters to make fun shapes which you can stick on to your pots.

⚠ Knives are sharp. Ask an adult to help you cut out the shapes.

Creating patterns

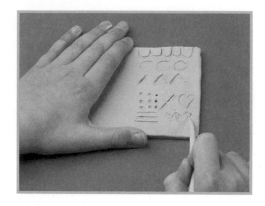

Wonderful patterns can be made in slabs of soft clay by rolling the clay over textured cloth or leaves, for example. Designs can be scratched into the surface with a modelling tool, the end of a pencil or even a stick. You can also impress objects into the clay to make patterns.

Joining and attaching

When joining coils or attaching small pieces of clay to larger pieces, the clay surfaces should be scored then moistened with water before being pressed and smoothed together. Allow all slab pieces to harden slightly first, so that they can be handled without losing their shape.

Note Pieces of air drying clay can be glued together with strong adhesive if you decide you want to add something to your model or pot after it is dry.

 Use a modelling tool to score (roughen) all the edges to be joined.

 Moisten the scored edges with a damp sponge.

 Press the two edges together firmly, then use your fingers or a modelling tool to smooth the joins.

 Finally, use a damp sponge on large pieces to create a really smooth finish.

Drying and painting

Before you paint your model, allow it to dry completely. The manufacturer's instructions will tell you how long you should wait, although it does depend on how warm your working environment is. If it is cold or damp, the drying time will be longer. Some instructions may tell you that you can speed up the process by drying the clay in the oven. This will harden the clay completely and make it more durable, but only do this if the instructions say so, and always get an adult to use the oven for you.

Acrylic paints are used for all the projects in this section. Poster paints can also be used, but you will need to seal them with acrylic varnish. The colours can be sponged on or you can use a brush to paint patterns and add fine details. An old toothbrush is ideal for spattering paint over surfaces. This creates lots of interesting effects, especially if you use several different colours.

Note Acrylic paints dry very quickly and paintbrushes and sponges must be cleaned immediately after use or they will be ruined.

Wobbly Pot

The pinching technique can be used to make a simple pinch pot like the one featured in this project. Throughout time, and in many different cultures, this style of pot has been used for various purposes. A good example is the diva pot used to hold small lights during the Hindu festival of Diwali.

YOU WILL NEED
Air-drying clay
Sponge
Modelling tool
Acrylic paints
Paintbrushes

 Use the pinching technique (see page 190) to create a simple pot shape.

 Squeeze the top of the pot to create a wavy edge. Leave it for half an hour to dry slightly.

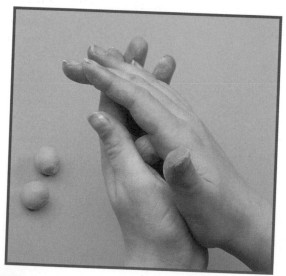

 Roll three small balls of clay.

 Score and moisten the surfaces to be joined (see page 192), then gently press each ball on to the base of the pot to form 'feet'. Smooth around the joins with a modelling tool. Leave to dry (see page 193).

5

Use a sponge to add large wavy stripes of paint around the pot.

6

Dip a stiff paintbrush or old toothbrush into acrylic paint, then hold it over the pot and rim and pull back the bristles with your finger. This will create a spattered paint effect. Wash your hands immediately afterwards.

FURTHER IDEAS

You can make wide and narrow pots — egg cups too. Decorate them with spots, stars or diamonds.

Fat Cat

In this project, coils of clay are used to make the collar, flower and tail for the cat. The eyes and ears are pinched out of small amounts of clay. Animal sculptures by the artist Picasso could be used as inspiration. You can model lots of animals by just squeezing and stretching the basic pinch pot. The cat can be changed into a penguin or a mouse in an instant!

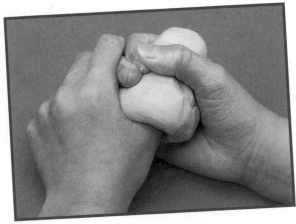

1 Make a basic pinch pot (see page 194). Turn it upside down and gently shape the head with your thumb.

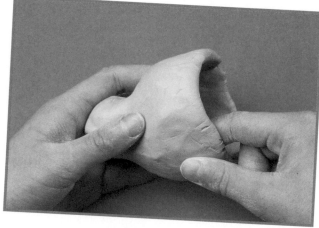

2 Squeeze the sides of the body, making it fatter than the head. Shape a nose and cheeks, then press in two eye sockets.

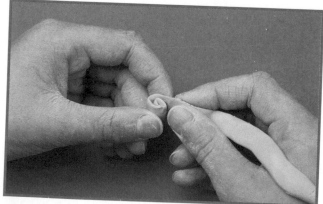

3 Roll out a coil of clay (see page 190) then flatten one end. Loosely spiral the flattened clay then pinch one end to form a flower head. Break off the flower then neaten the edge. Use the rest of the clay to make a collar and tail from coils, then two eyes and ears.

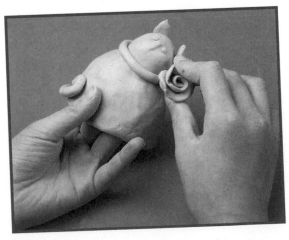

4 Attach the eyes, ears, tail and collar to the cat then add the flower to the collar (see page 192).

Use a pointed modelling tool to make a neat hole for the cat's mouth. Leave to dry.

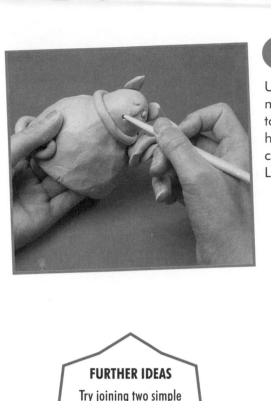

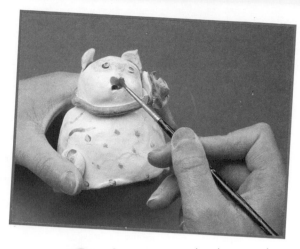

Sponge on a background colour and then use a paintbrush to add patterns to the body, the collar and the facial features.

FURTHER IDEAS
Try joining two simple pinch pots together and experiment to make other interesting animal models.

Swinging Tiger

Fun models like this tiger can be made from a solid lump of clay. Instead of pinching the clay into a pot shape, you simply roll it out and then pull out the arms and legs. Remember that the more clay you use, the longer it will take to dry. The smooth, pinched shapes of these models resemble the shapes of some African and Mexican sculpted creatures.

YOU WILL NEED

Air-drying clay
Modelling tool
Sponge • Acrylic paints
Paintbrushes
String or garden wire

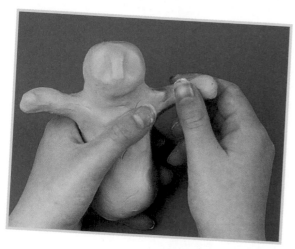

1 Roll out a fat clay sausage, shape a head and nose, then carefully pull two arms out from the sides of the body.

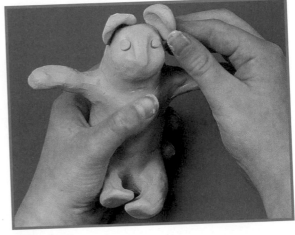

2 Model the bottom of the body and pull the legs out towards you. Add the eyes and ears.

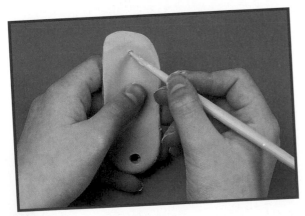

3 Model the swing seat from a slab of clay. Use the point of the modelling tool to make two small holes for the string or garden wire.

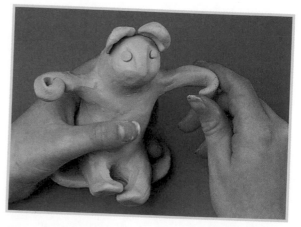

4 Attach the tiger to the seat. Bend the ends of its arms to form hands, leaving a hole in the middle of each for the string or garden wire to be pulled through. Leave to dry.

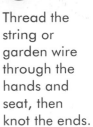

Thread the string or garden wire through the hands and seat, then knot the ends.

5 Sponge paint all over the model, then add stripes and facial features using a paintbrush.

FURTHER IDEAS

Try making your pet or even your best friend using this technique. You can add hair and facial features for people, then paint on colourful clothes.

Flower Pot

The technique of coiling is ideal for building up round symmetrical shapes like these flower pots. If you want your pot to be perfectly even, it is important to keep the coils the same thickness, and to continually turn the pot as you join and smooth the coils together. Look to artists and sculptors for ideas about what to paint on to or mould into the clay to decorate the flowerpot. Inspiration for the flowers could be taken from famous paintings such as Van Gogh's 'Sunflowers'.

YOU WILL NEED
Air-drying clay
Modelling tool • Pastry cutter
Garden or florist's wire
Pebbles • Moss
Acrylic paints
Paintbrushes

 Start to build up the walls of the pot using long, thin coils. Smooth the inside and outside surfaces with a modelling tool as you work upwards.

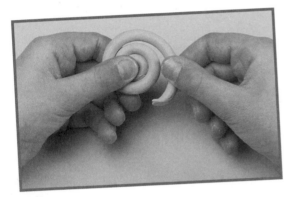

1 Roll out a coil of clay and use it to make a base. Smooth the coil flat.

3 When the pot is tall enough, smooth the top of the rim, then use part of a pastry cutter to create a fancy edge.

4 Roll out a piece of clay and use the technique shown on page 196 to make small flower heads. Squeeze pieces of clay between your fingers and model them to form longer flower heads.

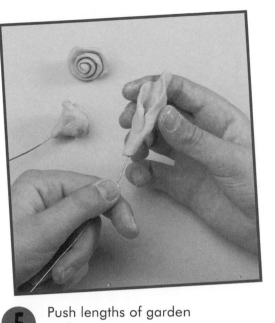

6 Paint the flowers and pot then leave to dry. Arrange the flowers in the pot and use small pebbles to hold the wire stems in position. Finally, cover the top of the pebbles with some moss.

5 Push lengths of garden or florist's wire into each flower head then leave to dry.

FURTHER IDEAS
Air-drying clay is not waterproof, but you could build up the coils around a small glass jar, so you can then fill it with water and real flowers.

Squiggly Bowl

Coil pots used to be made by ancient cultures such as Native Americans. The coils provide an instant decoration which can then be painted in vivid colours. By using different thicknesses of coil and varying the shape of the coil you can experiment to produce different patterns and textures. In this project, a bowl lined with clingfilm acts as a mould, and coils are built up on the inside of the bowl. You can use any shape as a mould, provided that the top is wider than its base so that it is easy to remove the finished piece.

YOU WILL NEED
Air-drying clay
Mould (bowl)
Clingfilm • Sponge
Modelling tool
Acrylic paints
Paintbrushes

1 Line the inside of the mould with clingfilm, then lay squiggles and coils of clay inside the bowl.

2 Join all the coils together by gently smoothing the inside surface with your fingers. Do not press too hard, as you want the coil pattern to remain on the outside.

3 Lay two long coils of clay around the top of the bowl to form a rim. Allow the pot to harden slightly before removing it from the mould.

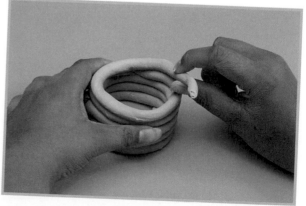

4 Make a base from long coils of clay. Smooth the inside of the coils together to make it stronger.

5 Turn the pot upside down and carefully attach the base (see page 192). Gently smooth the join with a modelling tool or your finger.

6 Allow the pot to dry completely, then paint the coils.

(see page 192)

FURTHER IDEAS

Make two bowls then place one on top of the other to make a person's head like the one shown here. You could also make a model of the Earth using this technique.

Fish Tile

The simple tile in this project is created by rolling the clay into a slab and then decorating it with cut-out shapes and paint. Look for different examples of tiles for inspiration. You may find them in your own home, or in most religious buildings. You can also look at the work of the Spanish artist, Gaudi, to see all the amazing things that can be done with tiles.

YOU WILL NEED
Air-drying clay
Knife • Rolling pin
Two lengths of wood • Sponge
Modelling tool • Acrylic paints
Paintbrushes • Scissors
Piece of wood

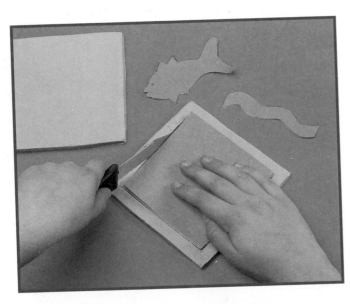

 1

Photocopy the square, border, fish and wave patterns on page 213. Cut them out and then place them on a slab of clay. Use a knife to cut around the shapes then set them aside and allow to harden slightly. Roll a few tiny balls of clay to form bubbles.

Knives are sharp. Ask an adult to help you cut out the shapes.

2 Attach the border to the square base (see page 192). Smooth the edges of the joins with a modelling tool.

3 Use a sponge to smooth over the edges further, and to smooth over the front of the border.

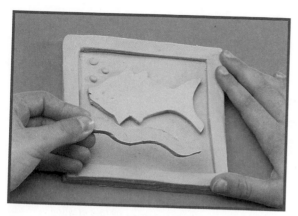

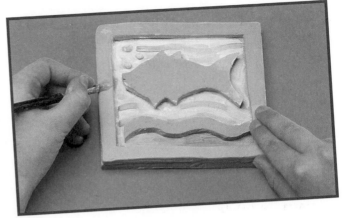

4 Attach all the pieces to the tile. Leave to harden slightly, then place a piece of wood on top to keep everything flat. Leave to dry thoroughly.

5 Paint the sea first, then apply a base colour to the fish, the wave and the border.

FURTHER IDEAS

You can use this technique to make a clock like the one shown here. Buy the clock mechanism first so that you know how big to make the hole in the clock face.

6 Use a paintbrush and different colours of paint to add details. Spatter on some speckles of paint with a stiff paintbrush or an old toothbrush.

Treasure Box

The decorations for this box are attached by scoring and moistening the two pieces of clay then joining them together. You could also explore other methods of decoration such as carving in shapes using modelling tools.

Photocopy the square patterns for the Treasure Box on page 213, then cut them out from slabs of clay. Allow the slabs to harden slightly then use a modelling tool to score the surfaces that will be joined.

 Knives are sharp. Ask an adult to help you cut out the shapes.

2 Moisten the edges with a sponge then assemble the box as shown, with the scored edges touching one another. Leave off one side for the moment. Pinch and squash the clay pieces together then smooth over the outer joins.

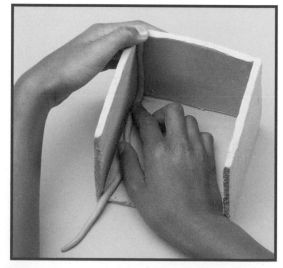

3 Roll out long thin coils, then press and smooth these over the inside joins to strengthen them. Attach the remaining side then carefully strengthen that with a coil.

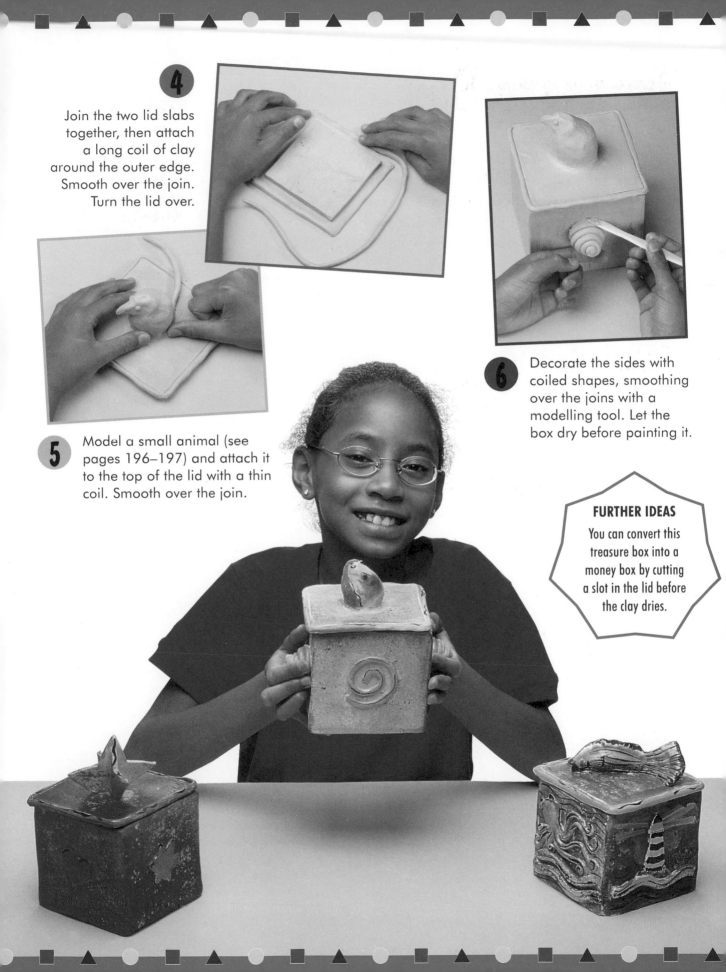

4

Join the two lid slabs together, then attach a long coil of clay around the outer edge. Smooth over the join. Turn the lid over.

5

Model a small animal (see pages 196–197) and attach it to the top of the lid with a thin coil. Smooth over the join.

6

Decorate the sides with coiled shapes, smoothing over the joins with a modelling tool. Let the box dry before painting it.

FURTHER IDEAS

You can convert this treasure box into a money box by cutting a slot in the lid before the clay dries.

Pencil Holder

Clay is an important material in the production of practical items, as well as being useful for producing decorative ornaments. The techniques used in this project are the same as those for the Treasure Box on pages 206–207, but the joins are strengthened on the outside rather than the inside.

YOU WILL NEED
Air-drying clay
Knife • Rolling pin
Two lengths of wood
Modelling tool
Pastry cutters • Sponge
Acrylic paints
Paintbrushes

1 Photocopy the patterns on page 212, then cut them out from slabs of clay. Allow the slabs to harden slightly, then assemble the triangle and three rectangles to form the basic pot shape.

Knives are sharp. Ask an adult to help you cut out the shapes.

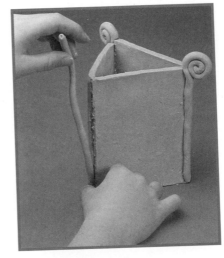

2 Roll out three long coils of clay, then smooth them on to the outside edges to strengthen the holder.

3 Decorate one side of the pencil holder using thin coils of clay to create windows, roof tiles, a door and even a milk bottle on the doorstep.

4 Use a coil and small pieces of clay to add a sunflower on one of the other sides. Use a pointed modelling tool to add veins to the leaves and seeds to the flower head.

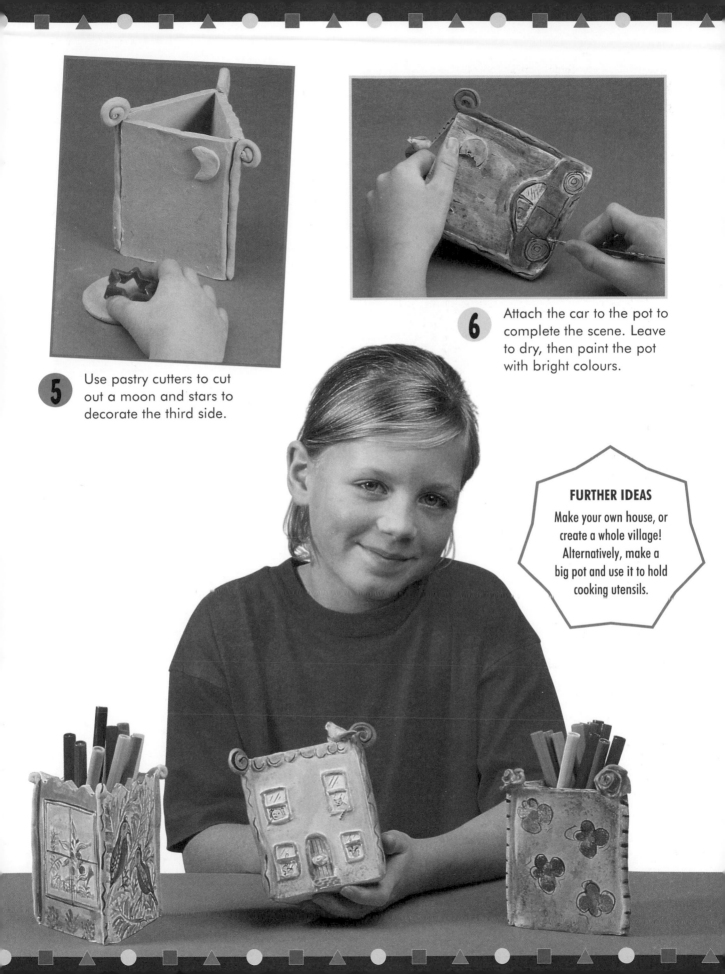

5 Use pastry cutters to cut out a moon and stars to decorate the third side.

6 Attach the car to the pot to complete the scene. Leave to dry, then paint the pot with bright colours.

FURTHER IDEAS

Make your own house, or create a whole village! Alternatively, make a big pot and use it to hold cooking utensils.

Lion Dish

Your imagination can really run wild with this dish. I show you how to make a lion, but all kinds of shapes can be produced to make a variety of fantastic creatures. Use a mixture of decorative techniques to finish it off, including moulding, attaching clay shapes or creating patterns using clay tools.

YOU WILL NEED
Air-drying clay
Rolling pin • Two lengths of wood
Mould (dish) • Clingfilm
Sponge • Modelling tool
Garlic press or sieve
Acrylic paints
Paintbrushes

1 Cover the mould with clingfilm. Roll out the clay, then lay it over the mould. Gently ease the clay down using a sponge.

2 Trim off excess clay with a modelling tool. Allow the clay dish to harden slightly, then remove it from the mould.

3 Model a head and tail then attach them to the rim of the dish. Shape two ears and attach them to the head. Smooth over the joins with your fingers.

4 Squeeze a ball of clay through a garlic press or sieve to create the lion's mane and tail.

5 Use a modelling tool to transfer the squeezed clay on to the end of the lion's tail and mane. Press the strands down well, then leave the dish to dry.

6 Sponge paint all over the dish. Use a paintbrush to add decoration and to colour in any areas that are hard to reach with a sponge.

FURTHER IDEAS
Use jelly moulds to create interesting shapes!
Look at animal books for interesting colours and patterns.

Patterns

The patterns on these two pages are the size that I used them for the projects, but you can make them larger or smaller on a photocopier if you wish. Once you have photocopied the patterns, you can cut them out and then place them over your clay and cut around the outline with a knife.

Get an adult to help you photocopy the patterns.

You will also need an adult to help you cut out the clay shapes.

Patterns for the Pencil Holder featured on pages 208–209. You will need three rectangular slabs of clay, one triangular slab and one car shape.

Patterns for the Fish Tile featured on pages 204–205. You will need two large square slabs of clay. Use one whole square for the background of the tile. Make the border from the other by cutting out the small square. Cut the fish and wave shapes from the remaining clay.

Patterns for the Treasure Box featured on pages 206–207. You will need five large square slabs for the actual box, and one large and one small square slab for the lid.

Beadwork

by Michelle Powell

Beads have been used for thousands of years in many different countries around the world. The earliest beads were found in the tombs of ancient Egyptians, and were made from semi-precious stones, shells, bone and gold. Beads were used not only as personal decoration but also as money. It became popular for people to carry their money beads on a string around their neck, to keep the beads safe, and to show how wealthy and important they were.

Certain types of beads also showed a person's religious or superstitious beliefs. The word bead comes from the Anglo-Saxon 'bede', meaning 'prayer'. People of many religions carry strings of rosary beads, each bead representing a prayer or psalm. Some people carry a talisman – a carved stone or other small object – believing that it will ward off evil spirits. Others wear a lucky charm, hoping that it will bring them good fortune.

Later, metal coins were used as currency. Some countries still have holes in their coins so that they can be strung together and worn as a necklace. Beads are now more normally used to make attractive jewellery and in craft projects like the ones in this section.

There are many different types of beads available. Some are made from beautiful gemstones dug from the ground such as garnet, turquoise and quartz. Amber beads are made from tree resins that have hardened in the ground for thousands of years. Precious metals such as gold and silver are also made into beads. Pearls are made in an oyster shell. This happens when a tiny grain of sand gets in to the shell. The oyster surrounds it with a special substance to make it smooth.

Many beads are made from glass. They are blown into shape or cut by highly skilled craftspeople. Wood and clay are also popular materials used to make beads. Plastic beads are made in lots of shapes and colours, using moulds.

This section shows you how to make many projects using beads and beading techniques. There are patterns at the end of the section to help you, and page 236 shows you how to transfer them on to your projects. You can make some of the beads yourself from air-drying clay, felt or high-density foam. Other projects use shop-bought beads such as tiny seed beads, larger plastic pony beads and even large polystyrene balls.

Bonsai Tree

In Japan, the art of growing tiny trees in shallow pots is called Bonsai. You can make your own miniature Bonsai trees, using sequins shaped like leaves and flower beads fastened on to wire branches. Fix the trees in some oasis and put them in small pots on your windowsill. You could make this spring tree covered in pink blossom, or use leaf beads or sequins in oranges, browns and reds for an autumnal tree.

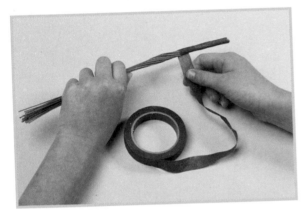

1 Using old scissors, cut thirty pieces of wire, 23cm (9in) long. Twist them together to half way along their length. Wrap brown flower tape around the twist. This makes the trunk of the tree.

Ask an adult to help you to cut the wire.

2 Split the bunch of wires into seven groups. Each group will make a branch of the tree. Twist the wires in each branch together to about half way along the branch.

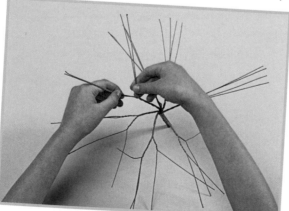

3 Divide each branch into two smaller branches. Twist the wires of the smaller branches together for a few centimetres. Leave wires sticking out in a 'v' shape at the end of each branch like twigs.

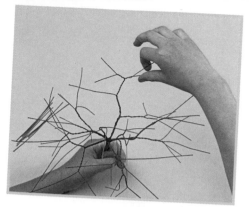

Ask an adult to help you to cut fourteen 5cm (2in) lengths of wire, using old scissors. Add them to the 'v' shapes at the ends of your branches. Twist them together with each side of the 'v', to thicken your twigs.

5

Take a flower bead and push a wire 'twig' through the hole. Push the bead 1cm (½in) down the twig. Bend back the end of the wire towards the centre of the flower. Now push a leaf sequin 1cm (½in) down another twig. Bend the wire over the top of the leaf and tuck it in round the back. Decorate the whole tree with flowers and leaves.

 Using a knife and a chopping board, carefully cut oasis to fit your pot and push it in. Push in your bonsai tree. Cover the top of the oasis with PVA glue, and sprinkle on gravel.

(!)

Ask an adult to help you to cut the oasis.

FURTHER IDEAS

Make a bonsai garden, or make a partridge from card and put it in a pear tree for Christmas.

Indian Wall Hanging

Traditional Indian clothes are made from bright fabrics in beautiful colours, often with shimmering metallic threads. This wall hanging is like an Indian decoration with its bright colours and shiny sequins. The stuffed felt beads are in the shape of birds, which often appear in Indian art and crafts. The small beads are rolled from strips of felt and decorated with felt in contrasting colours. Straws are used to make good holes through the beads so that they are easier to string together.

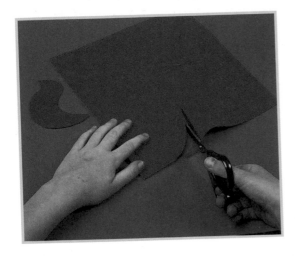

1 Transfer the bird design on page 237 on to card. Cut out the shapes and draw round them on felt, using a felt pen. Cut out two body shapes (front and back) and two wings for each bird. The wings should be in a contrasting colour.

2 Put a line of fabric glue around the edge of one back body piece. Lay a straw on the felt, and put cotton wool on top.

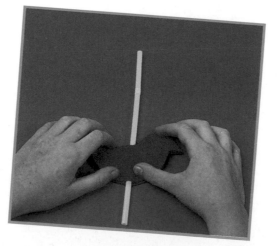

3 Push a front body piece on to the glue so the two halves of the bird stick together. Repeat steps 1–3 for four more birds.

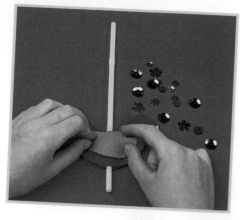

 4

Glue different coloured wings on to each bird. Glue on small triangles of yellow felt for beaks. Glue on sequins for decoration. Cut off the excess straw close to the felt.

 5

Cut thirteen strips of felt, 8cm (3¼in) long and 1cm (½in) wide. Cover one side with fabric glue and roll them around a straw to make felt beads. Leave to dry and then cut off the excess straw close to the felt.

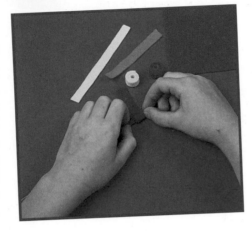

6

Use pinking scissors to cut strips of felt 5cm (2in) long and 5mm (¼in) wide. Glue them around your felt beads for decoration. Tie a bell on to a 60cm (23½in) piece of string. Push the string through the straws inside two felt beads. Next, thread a bird on to the string in the same way, then two more felt beads. Carry on until all the birds are on the string, then add three beads at the top.

FURTHER IDEAS

Design your own Indian style wall hanging using an elephant shape instead of a bird.

Egyptian Picture Frame

King Tutankhamen was a famous Egyptian pharaoh. After he died, a beautiful mask was made of his face and buried with him in his pyramid tomb. More than three thousand years later, archaeologists discovered this mask and many other buried treasures, which were signs of his wealth and importance as a leader. This picture frame uses small seed beads and long, straight bugle beads glued on to a wooden frame in a mosaic style, to create the look of King Tutankhamen's beautiful mask.

YOU WILL NEED
Wooden picture frame
Seed and bugle beads
Acrylic poster paint
Paint brush
PVA glue • Cocktail stick
Carbon paper • Tracing paper
Masking tape • Pencil

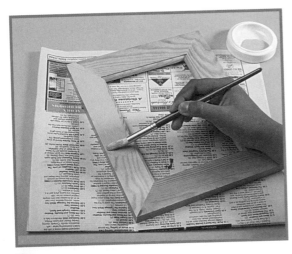

 Paint the picture frame a pale colour, using acrylic poster paint. Leave it to dry.

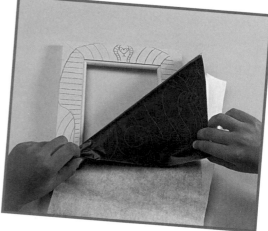

 Transfer the design on page 237 on to the frame.

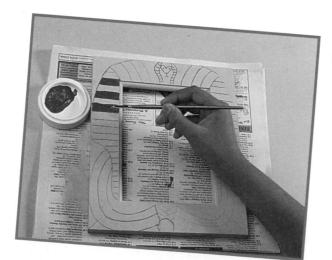

 Paint stripes of colour on to the frame as shown. Continue painting the design, leaving blank areas for beads between the colour.

4

Paint other areas of the design as shown and leave to dry. Put a line of glue on the design. Use a cocktail stick with a blob of glue on the end to pick up the long coloured bugle beads. Position the beads along the glued line.

5

Squeeze a thin layer of glue on to the unpainted semicircles at the bottom of the frame. Arrange the long gold beads, using the cocktail stick as before. Add glue to the unpainted striped areas and sprinkle on gold seed beads.

6

Press down the gold seed beads. Sprinkle on more to fill any gaps and leave the frame to dry.

FURTHER IDEAS
Design your own frame, and put in a picture inspired by the ancient Egyptians.

Fish Pen Toppers

Decorate your pens and pencils by making beaded fish and octopus toppers. The fish are made from a polystyrene ball, and sequins are used to look like the fish's scales. Small plastic faceted beads are used to make the fins and tail. Faceted beads are cut to have many flat faces or facets, like diamonds. This will give a shimmery feel to your fish. You could find some pictures of fish to copy or just use your imagination to create colourful fishy friends.

YOU WILL NEED
Pencil to decorate
Sequins • Beads
Thin wire • PVA glue
4cm (1½in) polystyrene balls
Scissors • Old scissors
Darning needle
Ruler

 Use the pencil to make a hole in the polystyrene ball.

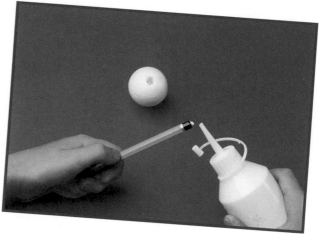

2 Glue the ball to the top of the pencil using PVA glue. Leave to dry.

3

Glue on a stripe of coloured sequins from the pencil hole, up and over the polystyrene ball and back to the pencil hole. Cover half of the ball with coloured sequins in the same way, and the other half with clear sequins. These will make the fish's face. Leave to dry.

4

Using old scissors, cut two 18cm (7in) lengths of wire. Thread twenty-five beads on one for the tail and twenty-five on the other for the fin. Bend the beaded wires into tail and fin shapes like those shown in the pattern on page 239.

Ask an adult to help you to cut the wire.

5

Make two holes in the ball with the darning needle where you want to add the fin. Put a blob of glue on each hole. Take the beaded fin and push one end of it into each hole. Do the same for the tail.

Ask an adult to help you to use the darning needle.

6

Place a blob of glue on either side of the face for the eyes and in the centre for the mouth. Push a black bead on to the glue for the eyes, and a clear bead for the mouth.

FURTHER IDEAS

Make beaded fish without the hole for a pencil. Attach magnets to the side to make fridge magnets.

African Beaded Curtain

The shapes and colours of this beaded curtain are taken from designs used to decorate African pottery. The leaves and curling vines look like the hanging canopy found in African forests. The beads are made from foam shapes and coloured drinking straws. Hang the curtain in the doorway of your bedroom, to give it an African theme.

YOU WILL NEED

High-density foam
Scissors • Large needle (bodkin)
Acrylic poster paint • Paint brush
Drinking straws • String
Pencil • Masking tape • Card
Tracing paper • Carbon paper
Wooden dowel the width of
your door

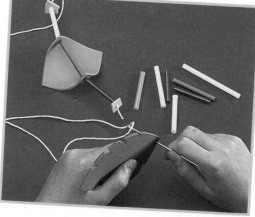

1 Transfer the patterns from page 238 on to card. Cut out leaf, triangle, star, zigzag and diamond templates. Draw round the templates on coloured foam.

2 Cut out eleven of each shape from the different coloured foam. Cut out eleven foam strips 30 x 2cm (11¾ x ¾in).

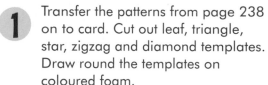

3 Paint the straws and cut them into various different lengths.

4 Cut the string into seven 2m (6½ft) lengths and thread one length on to the bodkin. Thread one end of a shape on to a string. Thread on a short piece of coloured straw, then thread on the other end of the shape. Thread a piece of straw in between each shape. Continue threading the shapes in this way.

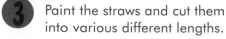

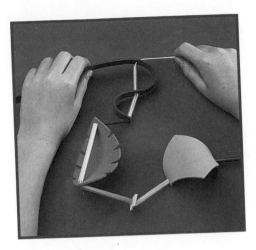

5 To thread the strips, make a small mark on the strip every 6cm (2¼in). Starting at one end, thread the needle and string through the strip, then through a short piece of straw, then again through the strip. Repeat to the end of the strip.

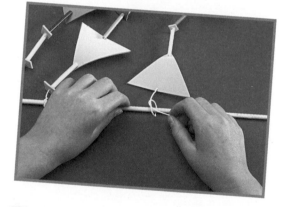

6 Thread shapes and straws on to all the strings. Tie the end of each string on to the dowel. The curtain is now ready to put up in your doorway.

Ask an adult to cut the dowel to the right length, and to hang the finished curtain for you.

FURTHER IDEAS
Decorate a foam band and put it round your head to make an African headdress.

Native American Shaker

Native Americans often made clothes and bags with a beaded tassel trim. Animal hide was cut into strips and threaded with beads for decoration. This shaker is made in a similar way, using felt cut into tassels, with pony beads threaded on to make a design. The felt is wrapped around a pot filled with more beads so that you can make music.

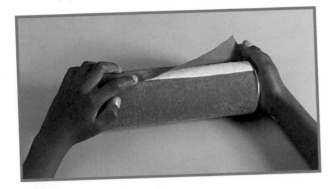

1 Cut a piece of fabric large enough to fit round the crisps pot. Cover the pot with PVA glue and leave until it is tacky. Glue the fabric on.

2 Cut two strips of felt, one 7cm (2¾in) wide and the second 18cm (7in) wide. Both must be long enough to go round the crisps pot. Draw lines 1cm (½in) apart on the strips. Cut fringes as shown, using the lines as a guide and cutting to 2cm (¾in) from the top.

3

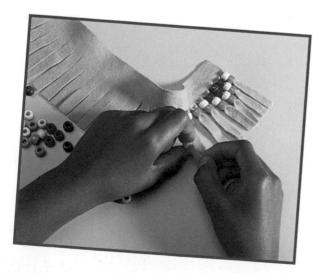

Thread beads on to the fringe of the smaller strip as shown, to make a pattern. Decorate the other fringe in the same way.

4

Glue the long fringe around the pot so that the tassels hang to the bottom of the pot. Glue the short fringe around the pot near the top.

5

Put any leftover beads into the pot to make the shaker noise.

6

Draw round the lid and cut out a circle of felt. Glue it on to the lid. Add a turquoise trim. Transfer the star and circle patterns on page 237 on to felt and cut them out. Stick the star on to the lid. Thread some decorative beads on to two 10cm (4in) pieces of string. Snip a tiny hole in the middle of the circle. Push the ends of the strings through the hole and glue the circle on top of the star.

FURTHER IDEAS
Make a fringed drum from a plastic tub to go with your shaker.

Gecko Key Ring

Geckos are lizards that live in warm countries. Their feet stick to smooth surfaces, so that they can run up walls and even across ceilings! These cute gecko key rings are great fun to make. Coloured pony beads are threaded on to string to form the shape of the gecko. You could use any beads, but make sure that the string you are using will pass easily through the bead hole twice. This technique is ideal for making reptiles like snakes, frogs or turtles, because the beads look like the patterns on scaly skin.

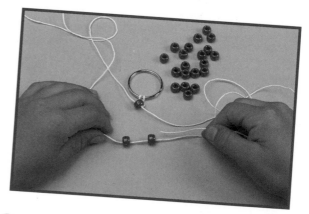

YOU WILL NEED
Eighty-five pony beads
Split ring
String
Scissors

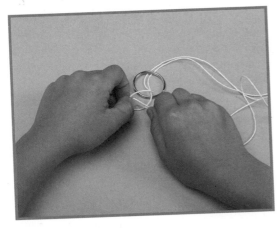

1 Cut 1m (39½in) of string. Fold it in half and loop it through the split ring. Push the two ends of the string through the loop and pull tight.

2 Look at the pattern on page 239. Thread one bead on to one of the strings, then push the other string through the bead in the opposite direction. Push the bead right up to the ring. Next thread two beads on to one string and thread the other string through in the opposite direction. Push both beads tight against the first bead.

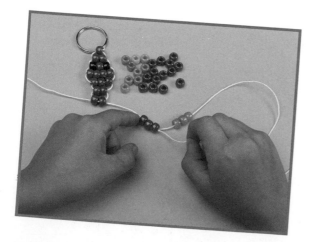

3 Continue following the pattern to make the gecko's head. Push the beads tight against each other after threading each row. To make the first leg, thread three dark and three light coloured beads on to one string. Bring the string round and thread it back through the dark beads.

 4

Make the second leg on the string on the other side. Now continue with the body, following the pattern. Pull the strings tight after threading on each row of beads.

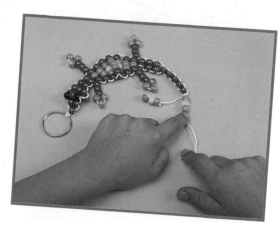

 5

Make the gecko's back legs in the same way as the front legs. Next thread two beads on to the string on one side, and then thread the other string through the beads in the opposite direction. Continue following the pattern in the same way to make the tail.

 6

Tie off the strings together at the end of the tail. Now thread three more beads on to each remaining length of string, for decoration. Knot and cut off both strings.

FURTHER IDEAS
Make zip pulls or a mobile with your beaded creatures, or use glow in the dark beads to make aliens or ghosts!

Rainbow Sun Catcher

This sun catcher's pattern is in the shape of a traditional stained-glass window. The stained-glass windows in churches show scenes from the Bible. In times when many people could not read, preachers used them to teach people about Bible stories. For this sun catcher, you need pony beads that are coloured but transparent, so that the light will shine through them, as well as some opaque beads. The beads are threaded on to strings, so that when they are hung together, they will form a picture of the sun rising, a rainbow and a moonlit sky, all in a window frame. Stick your sun catcher to your window, and wait for some sunshine to bring it to life!

YOU WILL NEED
Black and metallic opaque pony beads
Clear, coloured pony beads
A kebab stick
Three window suckers
Ruler • Scissors
String

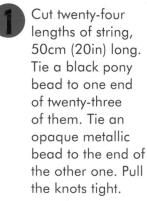

1 Cut twenty-four lengths of string, 50cm (20in) long. Tie a black pony bead to one end of twenty-three of them. Tie an opaque metallic bead to the end of the other one. Pull the knots tight.

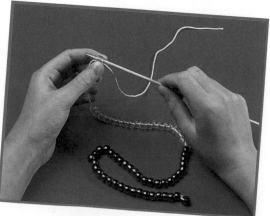

2 Look at the pattern on page 239. Using the first string, thread the opaque metallic beads and the clear beads in column one. Thread the last clear bead on to the string.

3 Now thread this last clear bead on to the kebab stick. Tie the string round the kebab stick and cut off the end of the string.

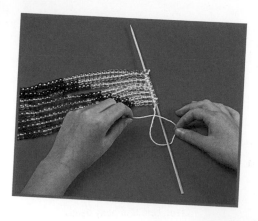

Carry on threading beads on to the strings, one column at a time, following the pattern. Push the kebab stick through each final bead and tie the string round the kebab stick as shown.

Continue following the pattern, tying off the ends and cutting off the excess string.

Hook three window suckers on to the kebab stick. Now the sun catcher is ready to be attached to your window.

FURTHER IDEAS
Add bells to the bottom of the sun catcher and hang it up to make a wind chime.

Astronaut Puppet

Polystyrene balls can be used as huge beads and strung together to make an astronaut puppet wearing a space suit. You will need polystyrene balls in the following shapes and sizes: two 8cm (3¼in) egg shapes for the hands; two 10cm (4in) egg shapes for the feet; one 9cm (3½in) ball for the head; one 11cm (4¼in) ball for the body; two 6cm (2¼in) balls for the shoulders; four 8cm (3¼in) balls for the legs, and four 7cm (2¾in) balls for the arms and legs.

1 Use a kebab stick to push a hole straight through the middle of all the polystyrene balls except the body. Make three holes in the body as shown, and then pull out the kebab sticks.

> **(!)** Ask an adult to help you to make holes with the kebab sticks.

2 Paint two of the egg shapes as gloves, and the other two as space boots. Paint the details of the face and helmet and the body. Paint the polystyrene block. This will be the astronaut's oxygen tank.

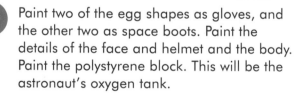

3 Make a long needle by twisting the end of a piece of wire as shown. Thread it with elastic thread. Tie a knot, then thread on a small bead, a glove, two arm beads, the body and then another two arm beads, the other glove and a second small bead. Then tie another knot.

Thread another piece of elastic thread through a small bead, a boot and three leg beads. Push the needle up through one of the body holes, then down through the second hole. Thread on three more leg beads, a boot and a bead, and tie a knot.

4

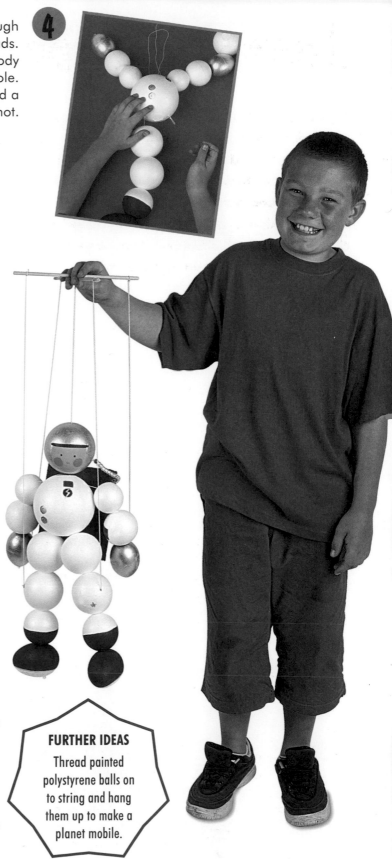

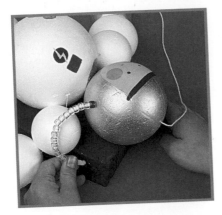

5 Thread a piece of elastic thread down through the head bead and tie it to the loop left by the legs. Stick the oxygen tank to the body using PVA glue. Thread some clear beads on to a pipe cleaner, and push one end in the helmet and the other end in the oxygen tank.

6 Make small wire hooks and stick them in the knees and hands, then tie on four lengths of string 75cm (29½in) long. Tie the other ends to the two pieces of wooden dowel, tied in a cross shape. Put another wire hook in the head, and use string to attach it to the centre of the dowel cross.

FURTHER IDEAS
Thread painted polystyrene balls on to string and hang them up to make a planet mobile.

Aztec Game

The Aztecs lived in Mexico around five hundred years ago. They were warlike people but they also made amazing art and crafts. They carved the shapes of faces and animals in to tall wooden poles, to make sculptures. This game is based on Aztec sculptures. The playing pieces are large clay beads in the shapes of birds and faces. You need fourteen birds and fourteen faces to play three-dimensional noughts and crosses.

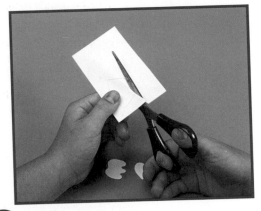

1 Transfer the tail, feet and wing patterns on page 238 on to card and cut them out to make templates.

2 Roll twenty-eight balls of clay the size of a walnut in your hands. Use the straw to make a hole through the middle of each ball.

3 Roll out a piece of clay about 4mm (¹/₈ in) thick and use the templates to cut out wing, feet and tail shapes for the birds. Stick these to fourteen of the clay beads.

234

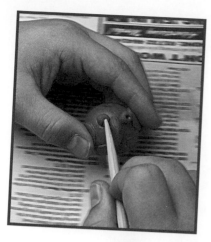

 4

Roll balls for the eyes. Press them on to the clay beads, using a little water to help them stick. Use a clay cutting tool to indent the eyeballs and make grooves in the wings and tails. Leave to dry.

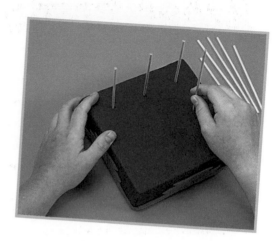

 5

Paint the fourteen bird beads and leave them to dry. Now make fourteen Aztec face beads using the face pattern on page 238. Paint them, too.

6

Take the square of polystyrene and cover it with felt. Use the pattern on page 238 to make a felt decoration for each side. Push the pieces of dowel into the square in evenly spaced rows of three. Now you can play three-dimensional noughts and crosses with the birds and face beads – any straight line of three beads wins!

FURTHER IDEAS
Make a draughts board from card and use your beads to play draughts.

Transferring Patterns

You can trace the patterns on these pages straight from the book (step 1). Alternatively, you can make them larger or smaller on a photocopier if you wish, and then follow steps 2–4 to transfer them on to your project.

> **(!)** Get an adult to help you enlarge the patterns on a photocopier.

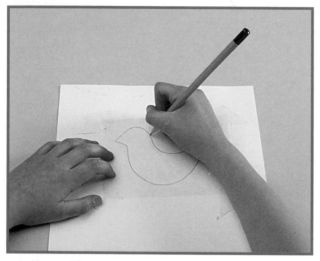

1 Place a piece of tracing paper over the pattern, then tape it down with small pieces of masking tape. Trace around the outlines using a soft pencil.

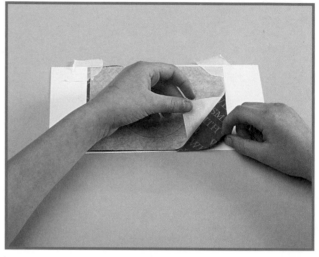

2 Place the tracing paper or photocopy on the surface of the project and tape it at the top. Slide the carbon paper underneath and tape it at the bottom.

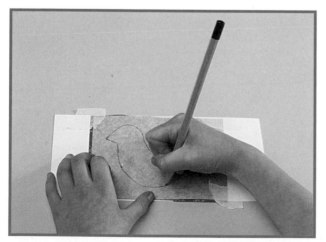

3 Trace over the outlines with the pencil, pressing down firmly.

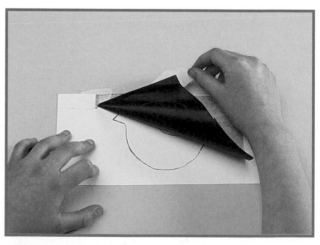

4 Remove the tracing paper, and the carbon paper, to reveal the design.

Patterns

Patterns for the
Indian Wall Hanging
featured on pages
218–219

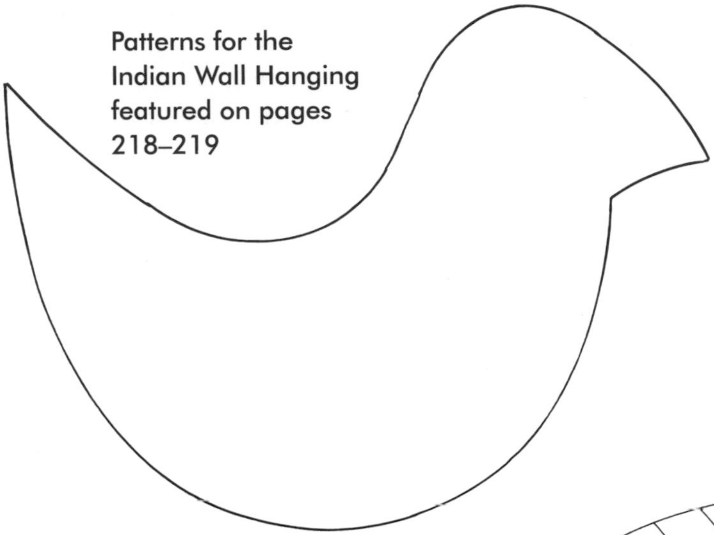

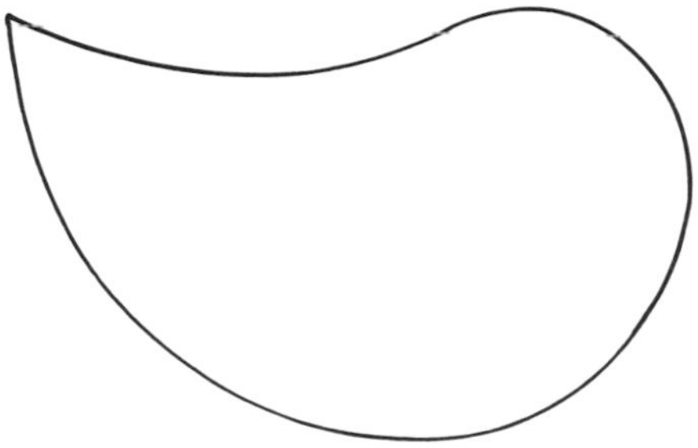

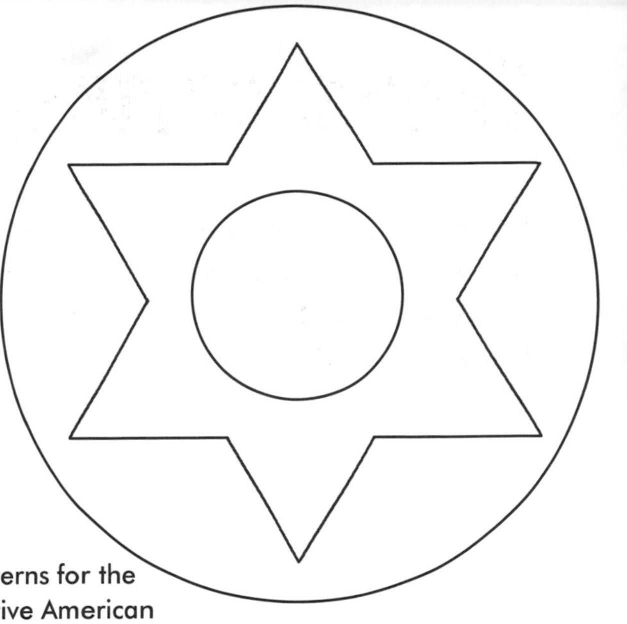

Patterns for the
Native American
Shaker featured on pages 226–227

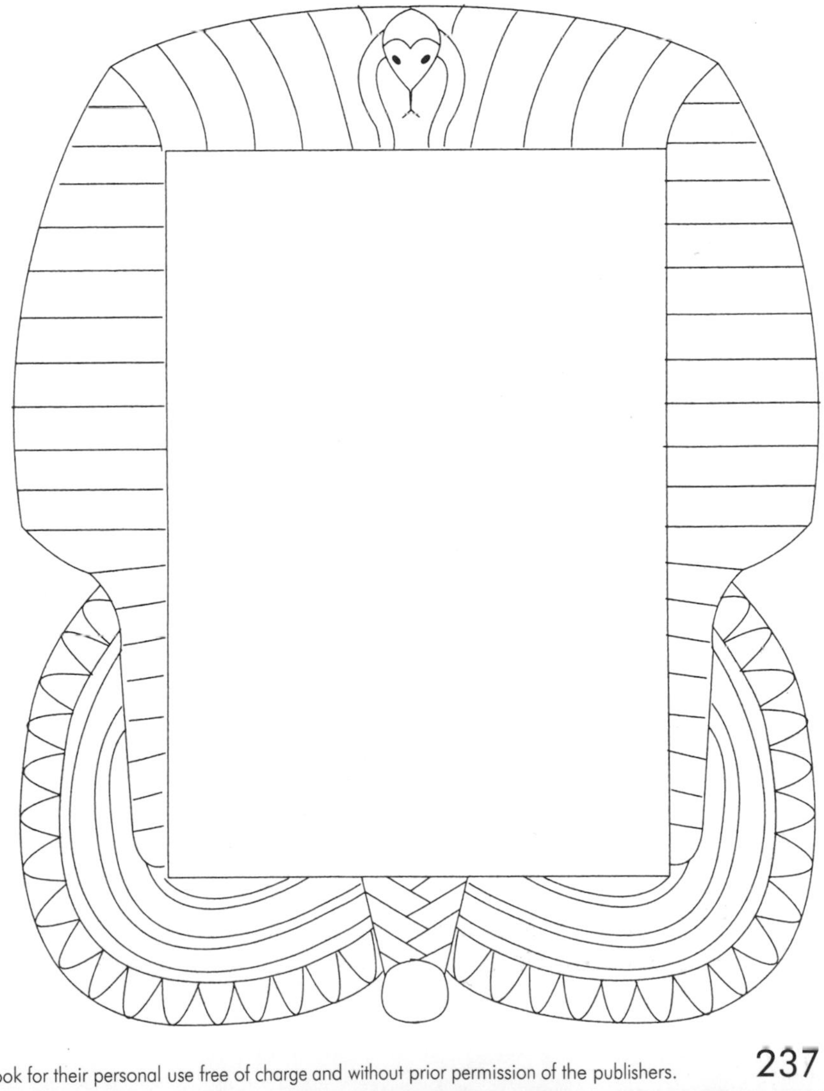

Pattern for the Egyptian
Picture Frame featured on
pages 220–221

Patterns for the African
Beaded Curtain featured on
pages 224–225

Patterns for the Aztec Game featured on pages 234–
235. Top left to right: tail, feet, wing and face patterns.
Bottom: felt decoration for the base.

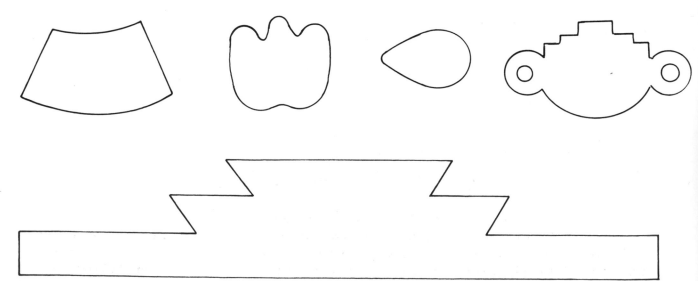

Pattern for the Rainbow Sun Catcher featured on pages 230–231

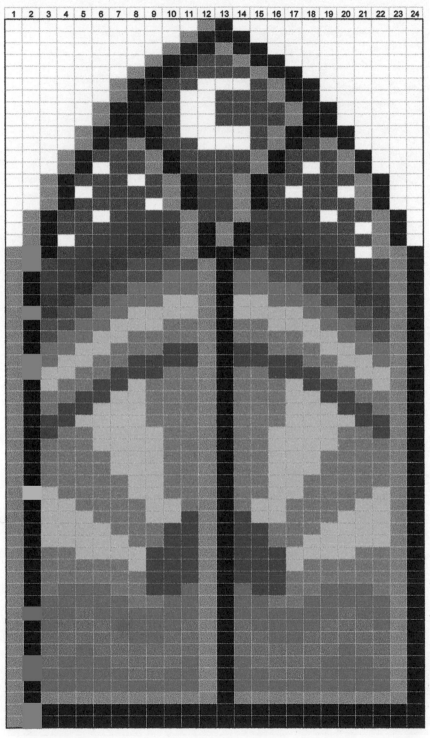

| 1 | 2 | 3 | 4 | 5 | 6 | 7 | 8 | 9 | 10 | 11 | 12 | 13 | 14 | 15 | 16 | 17 | 18 | 19 | 20 | 21 | 22 | 23 | 24 |

You will need: 237 opaque black beads; 190 opaque metallic beads (shown as grey); 128 clear turquoise beads; 68 clear red beads; 90 clear green beads; 194 clear orange beads; 140 clear yellow beads; 32 clear purple beads; 34 clear pink beads; 95 clear blue beads and 208 clear colourless beads.

Patterns for the Fish Pen Toppers featured on pages 222–223

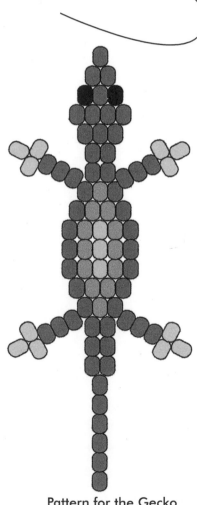

Pattern for the Gecko Key Ring featured on pages 228–229

Decorative Painting

by Judy Balchin

So what exactly is meant by decorative painting? Well, let us try to imagine a world where it does not exist – where all surfaces are plain with no decoration. Difficult, isn't it? For thousands of years, people have had an irresistible desire to decorate things, from cave walls and pottery to buildings, furniture and fabrics. Throughout history we have been attracted to pattern and colour, and today you only have to look around your own home, or visit your local shopping centre, to see a wonderful variety of decorative colours and shapes.

Before starting the projects in this section, take a little time to look at the types of decoration used by different civilisations and countries. Each one has its own colour preferences and style. This can be seen when you look at floral designs. Flowers have always been popular as a subject, but compare the simple, stylish Lotus flower designs of ancient Egyptian artists with the intricate blossoms created by the Chinese. Both are beautiful, but very different.

You do not have to look far to find things to decorate and you do not have to spend a lot of money on them. We use flowers to decorate a box in the following pages, but we also have great fun decorating eggs with monsters and pebbles with animals. Wooden spoons are decorated with insects and colourful patchwork squares are painted on a glass jar to transform it into a fancy sweet container.

I will show you how to paint on different surfaces, including wood, paper, cardboard, terracotta, glass and stone. All the objects can be found easily, in or around your home. Cardboard boxes, paper plates, used containers and many other objects can be transformed with a little paint and some imagination. Acrylic paints have been used in every project, as these are inexpensive, cover the surface and are hard-wearing.

I have had great fun writing this section, and hope that as you work through the projects you will think of other ways of decorating surfaces. Look out for unusual things to paint. Be bold with your designs, use bright colours and have lots of fun!

Techniques

Decorative painting is not difficult to do, but it is worth reading through this section carefully before you start. The techniques are demonstrated on a cardboard box. Always clean brushes thoroughly in water after using them.

Note Decorative painting can be messy so it is best to cover your work surface with a large piece of newspaper.

Painting

Use a flat brush to paint large surfaces. This gives an even finish which is easier to work on. Sometimes, you may need to apply two coats of paint, so the surface is well covered. Allow the first coat to dry before applying the second.

Splattering

Protect the work surface with newspaper. Dilute some paint on a palette with water so that it is runny. Dip the bristles of a toothbrush in the paint. Hold the toothbrush with the bristles towards the surface you are decorating and run your finger along the brush. This will splatter random paint spots on to the surface.

Masking and sponging

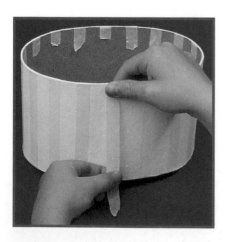

To mask areas of an object, press strips of masking tape on to the surface. Make sure that the edges of the tape are smoothed flat. The masked areas will remain the base colour.

When sponging, pour a little paint on to a palette. Dip the sponge in the paint, then dab the surfaces of the base and lid all over. Remove the masking tape to reveal neat stripes.

Stencilling, painting and outlining

Now that the surfaces have been prepared with flat colour and textured effects, images can be added. Stencils are a quick and easy way to create pictures which can then be added to and outlined.

1 Tape the stencil to the surface with small pieces of masking tape. Use a sponge to dab the paint through the stencil. Remove the stencil.

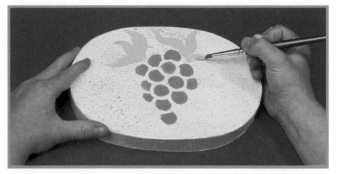

2 Paint in the pattern using a small paintbrush. Pull the brush towards you smoothly, lifting it off the surface as you complete the stroke to create a neat shape.

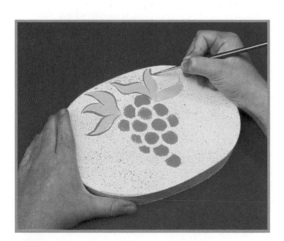

3 Outlining with black paint makes images really stand out. For this design, use a small round paintbrush to outline the leaves and the left-hand side of the grapes. This will create a three-dimensional effect.

Bumble Bee Spoon

The insect world is fascinating and amazing. Think of the bee, the ladybird and the butterfly – they are all so different. Their amazing range of shapes and colours is not accidental. The insects use them as a defence against enemies and to attract other insects. In this project a bee motif is used to decorate a wooden spoon, and the same colours are used on the handle. Wood is a wonderfully smooth surface to paint on. If your spoon is a little rough, sand it down with sandpaper before starting.

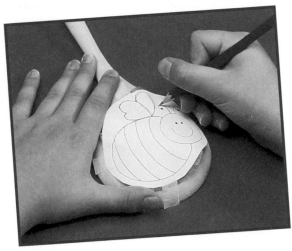

1 Transfer the pattern on page 263 on to the back of the spoon (see page 262).

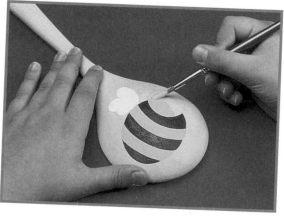

2 Paint the black stripes and then paint the bee's body and head using a small paintbrush and a light colour. Leave to dry.

3 Paint the bee's cheeks, then carefully outline the bee in a dark colour. Paint in the eyes, mouth and antennae.

4

Paint the handle in the lighter colour. When it is dry, paint in the darker stripes.

5

Use a larger paintbrush to varnish the back of the spoon. When the varnish is dry, turn the spoon over and repeat on the front.

6

Tie a coloured ribbon around the handle so that you can hang it up.

Note This bumble bee spoon is purely decorative and should not be used to cook or eat with.

FURTHER IDEAS
Copy paintings of other brightly coloured insects and make your own colony of insect spoons.

Rosy Gift Box

Artists have painted and decorated surfaces with flowers for a long time, inspired by the beautiful colours and shapes they have found in nature. Many fine examples of flower paintings can be found in museums and art galleries. These simple roses are easy to paint. They are used to transform a plain cardboard container into a lovely gift box. Look for an old box to decorate – you do not have to buy one.

YOU WILL NEED

Cardboard box
Black acrylic paint
Coloured acrylic paint
Large and small paintbrushes
Sponge • Palette

 Use a large brush to paint the box and lid with a pale colour. You may need to apply two coats if the first one does not cover the surface completely. Make sure that the first coat is dry before applying the second.

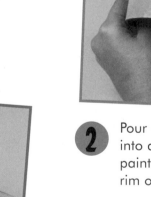

 Pour a small amount of a darker colour into a palette. Dip the sponge in the paint and dab it around the base and rim of the lid. Leave to dry.

3 Using a smaller brush and the same colour, paint circles all over the lid and box. Leave to dry.

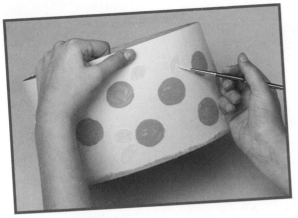

4 Paint leaf shapes around the circles using a different colour. Try to fill in any gaps. Leave to dry.

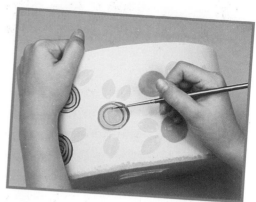

5 Decorate each coloured circle with a large swirl using black paint and a small paintbrush. Allow to dry.

6 Outline the leaves with black paint and add a vein line down the centre of each one.

FURTHER IDEAS

Decorate boxes with different flowers – daisies, sunflowers and poppies. Keep the designs simple and use bright colours.

Sun Wall Hanging

Astrology is the study of the Sun, Moon, planets and stars, and the way they influence our lives. Astrological symbols have been used as decoration by artists and craftspeople throughout the ages. The Sun is ninety-three million miles away from Earth, but you can bring it right into your own home by creating this colourful Sun wall hanging. A paper plate is the perfect round blank on which to work. The basic design is painted and then decorated with dots and swirls of metallic paint.

Note Place your plate over a roll of masking tape. This will help support the plate when you are painting it.

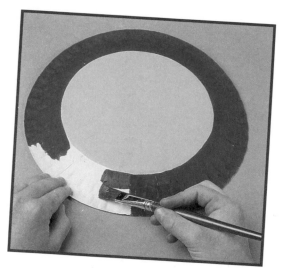

 Using a large paintbrush, paint the centre of the plate in a light colour and the border in a dark colour. Leave to dry.

2 Transfer the pattern on page 263 on to the centre of the plate (see page 262). Using a small paintbrush, outline the features in a dark colour, then paint in the eyes and cheeks. Leave to dry.

 Paint the eyebrows, eyelids, lips and chin with a lighter colour. Allow to dry.

 4 Use a pencil to draw the Sun's rays around the border. Carefully cut them out.

 5

Decorate the Sun's face with dotted swirls of metallic paint. Add dotted swirls to the rays. Leave to dry.

 6 Tape a loop of string to the back of the top ray so that you can hang up your Sun.

FURTHER IDEAS

Make Moon and star wall hangings to complement your Sun – or decorate lots of small plates and create a matching mobile.

Patchwork Sweet Jar

For generations, people have created patchwork using scraps and odd remnants of material. You may have seen beautifully stitched quilts made in this way. They are usually made to commemorate an event or special occasion, such as a wedding. In this project we use paint to create our own patchwork. An old glass jar is decorated and transformed into a stylish sweet container. Look for a large jar to show off your painting. Do not forget to wash and dry it thoroughly before you begin.

YOU WILL NEED
Large glass jar
Black and white acrylic paint
Coloured acrylic paint
Large and small paintbrushes
Pencil • Varnish • Sweets
Coloured fabric • Scissors
Elastic band
Coloured ribbon

Paint the jar with two coats of white paint using a large brush. Leave an unpainted square in the middle, so when the jar is finished you can see what is in it. Let the first coat of paint dry before applying the second coat.

Use a pencil to divide the jar up into squares.

Paint the neck of the jar using a large paintbrush and a bright colour. When the jar is dry, paint in the squares using different colours. Leave to dry.

5 Add stitch lines around each square using a fine paintbrush and black paint. Leave to dry, then paint a coat of varnish on to the jar using a large brush.

4 Decorate each square with dots, lines or hearts. Try to make each one different.

FURTHER IDEAS

Recycle old bottles and create colourful patchwork patterns on them — or decorate other glass objects.

6 Fill the jar with sweets. Cut out a circle of fabric double the size of the top of the jar. Secure the fabric around the top with an elastic band. Finally, tie a ribbon over the elastic band.

Padlocked Money Box

This project uses *trompe l'oeil*, a French term that means 'deception of the eye'. It refers to something that looks real, but is not – it is just an illusion. The padlock and chain on this money box look real, but they are just painted on. Painted shadow lines and highlights make them look three-dimensional.

YOU WILL NEED
Cardboard tube with plastic lid
Black and white acrylic paint
Metallic acrylic paint
Large and small paintbrushes
Toothbrush • Palette • Tracing paper
Transfer paper • Masking tape
Pencil • Newspaper
Craft knife • Cutting mat

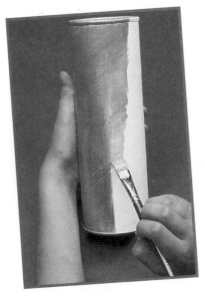

1 Paint the tube with white paint using a large brush and allow it to dry. You may have to apply a few coats of paint to cover any lettering. Wait for the last coat to dry, then apply two coats of metallic paint.

2 Cover the work surface with sheets of newspaper. Lay the tube on top. Pour small amounts of black and white paint into a palette and dilute them both with water. Using a toothbrush, splatter the tube first with white, then with black paint (see page 242). Roll the tube to make sure that you splatter the whole surface.

3 Transfer the pattern on page 264 on to the tube and fill it in with metallic paint. Leave to dry.

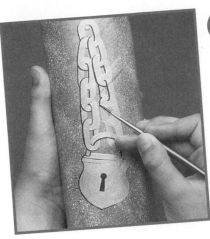

4 Using a small paintbrush, paint the keyhole. Add black shadow lines down the left-hand side and along the bottom of the chain links and padlock. Leave to dry.

5

Paint white lines down the right-hand side and along the tops of the links and padlock, to create highlights.

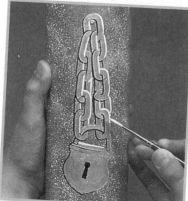

6 Cut a slot in the top of the lid with a craft knife, then place the lid on top of the tube.

(!)

A craft knife is very sharp; it should always be used with a cutting mat. Ask an adult to help you.

FURTHER IDEAS

Design some symbols that mean 'Keep out', 'Private', 'Danger' and use these to decorate your money box.

Tiger Paperweight

Decorating pebbles or stones is an unusual and fascinating craft, and it is easy to do. Part of the fun is finding just the right shape. Look for a pebble or stone that suggests the shape of a tiger, and make sure that it has a smooth surface, as this will be easier to paint. Keep your design simple and use bold colours for the best effect.

YOU WILL NEED

Pebble
White and black acrylic paint
Coloured acrylic paint
Large and small paintbrushes
Pencil • 2 plastic eyes
PVA glue

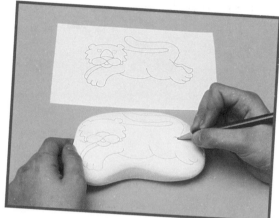

1 Paint the pebble white using a large paintbrush. Leave to dry. Copy the pattern from page 264 on to the pebble using a pencil.

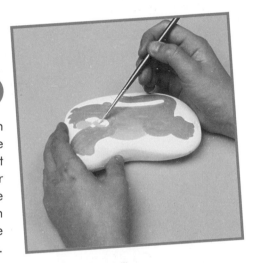

2 Using an appropriate colour, paint in the darker areas of the body, then paint in the lighter areas.

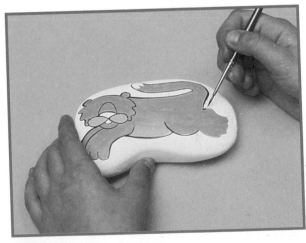

3 Outline the tiger using a small paintbrush and black paint.

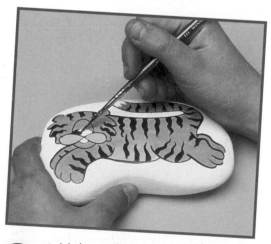

4 Add the stripes, nose and mouth using a small paintbrush and black paint. Leave to dry.

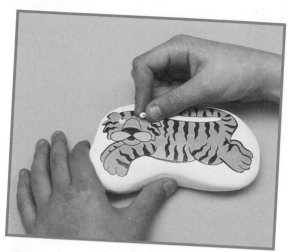

5 Glue on the plastic eyes using PVA glue. Leave to dry.

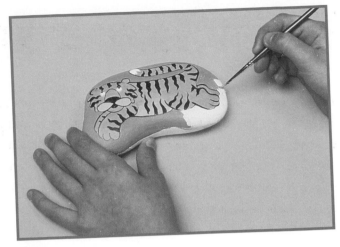

6 Paint the rest of the pebble in a bright colour. Leave to dry.

FURTHER IDEAS
Look for pebbles with unusual shapes and create your own animals and birds.

Fruity Flower Pot

Artists and craft workers have always used fruit motifs as decoration because of the amazing variety of shapes and colours they offer. Try making a list of all the fruits you can think of, and you will soon realise what a wonderful choice there is – oranges, apples, strawberries, lemons, grapes and more! This fruity project combines masking with sponging and stencilling – easy techniques that transform a plain terracotta pot into a colourful decorative plant container. Use an inexpensive sponge and tear pieces off as you need them.

YOU WILL NEED
Terracotta pot
Coloured acrylic paint
Large paintbrush • Palette
Thin card • Tracing paper
Transfer paper
Narrow masking tape
Pencil • Sponge • Scissors
Old cloth

 Paint the pot in a light colour using a large paintbrush. Leave to dry. Apply vertical strips of masking tape around the pot (see page 242). Try to make the gaps between the strips the same.

Pour some darker coloured paint into a palette and sponge the unmasked stripes (see page 242). Carefully remove the masking tape and leave to dry.

Carefully sponge the top of the rim and the base of the pot with a different colour.

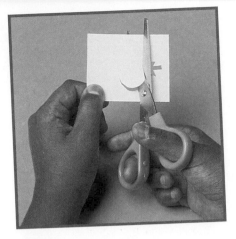

5

Lay the pot down on an old cloth to stop it rolling around. Tape the stencil on to the pot with masking tape.

4

Transfer the strawberry pattern on page 263 on to thin card. Cut out the strawberry shape to create a stencil.

6

Sponge paint through the stencil on to the pot. Choose two appropriate colours and use two pieces of sponge to colour the top of the strawberry, then the fruit. Work around the pot varying the angle of the strawberries.

FURTHER IDEAS

Change your designs by painting horizontal stripes around your pot and choose other types of fruit.

Monster Egg

An artist called Carl Fabergé created beautifully decorated eggs in the late nineteenth century. Some of his more precious jewelled eggs were made for the Russian royal family. I have used a hard boiled egg for this project and created an optical illusion. Although the monster is painted on the surface of the egg, it looks as though he is living inside it! If you want projects to last a long time, polystyrene or papier mâché eggs can be decorated using the same techniques.

! Ask an adult to boil the egg for you before you start the project.

1 Paint the top half of the egg in a colour of your choice using a large paintbrush. Sit it in an egg cup and leave it to dry. Turn it over and paint the bottom half. Leave to dry. Take care not to get paint on the egg cup.

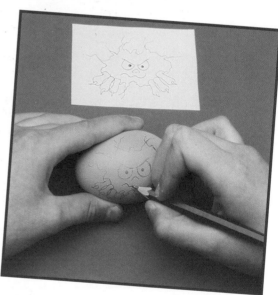

2 Copy the monster pattern from page 264 on to the egg using a pencil.

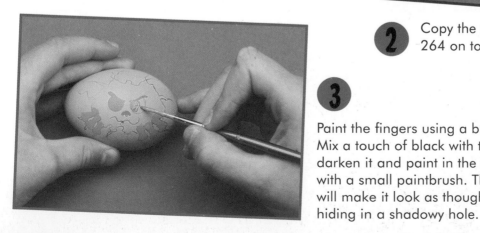

3 Paint the fingers using a brighter colour. Mix a touch of black with this colour to darken it and paint in the nose and eyes with a small paintbrush. The darker colour will make it look as though the monster is hiding in a shadowy hole.

4 Add the claws, mouth and staring eyes using another bright colour.

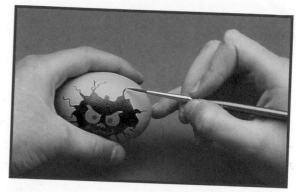

5 Fill in the area behind the monster's features using black paint. Outline the fingers with the same paint, then add the lines around the edge of the hole.

6 Paint a thin white line along one side and along the bottom of the hole. Paint small white dots at the base of the fingers. This gives the appearance of highlights which makes the monster look even more three-dimensional.

FURTHER IDEAS
Use metallic acrylic paints to create realistic alien eggs, or invent your own monster.

Picasso Mirror

This project is inspired by the work of the Spanish artist, Pablo Picasso. He was born in 1881 and was one of the greatest painters of the twentieth century. You can use the style and colours of his work to create your own masterpiece. Before you start, take time to look at Picasso's work.

Transfer the pattern from page 265 on to card (see page 262). Using bright colours and a small paintbrush, start filling in the design.

Continue painting the frame until all the areas are filled in.

Outline the design using black paint. Leave to dry. Cut off the outer unpainted border using a craft knife. Cut out the unpainted central section.

A craft knife is very sharp and it should always be used with a cutting mat. Make sure you ask an adult to help you when you use it.

Paint the outside and inside edges of the cut card black.

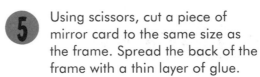

5 Using scissors, cut a piece of mirror card to the same size as the frame. Spread the back of the frame with a thin layer of glue.

6

Carefully press the frame down on to the mirror card, matching all the corners. Leave to dry.

Note While the glue is drying, place a heavy book on top of the frame to prevent warping.

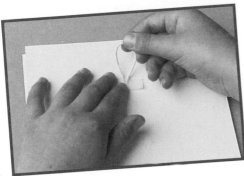

7 Tape a loop of string to the back of the frame with masking tape, so that you can hang up your mirror.

FURTHER IDEAS

Look at the work of other famous artists. Decorate photograph frames or mirror frames in their style.

Patterns

You can trace the patterns on these pages straight from the book (step 1). Alternatively, you can make them larger or smaller on a photocopier if you wish, and then follow steps 2–4.

Ask an adult to help you enlarge the patterns on a photocopier.

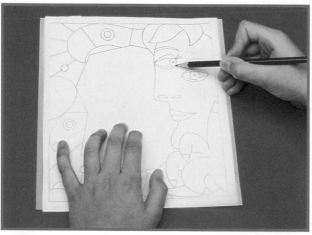

1 Place a piece of tracing paper over the pattern, then tape it down with small pieces of masking tape. Trace around the outlines using a soft pencil.

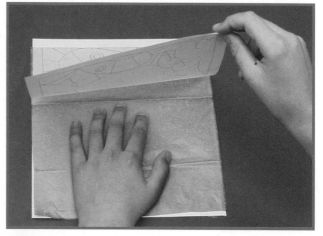

2 Place the tracing paper or photocopy on the surface of the project and tape it at the top. Slide the transfer paper underneath and tape it at the bottom.

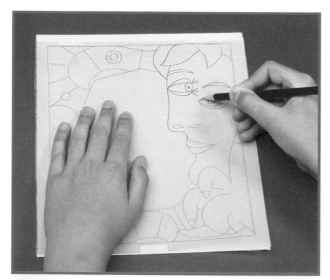

3 Trace over the outlines with the pencil, pressing down firmly.

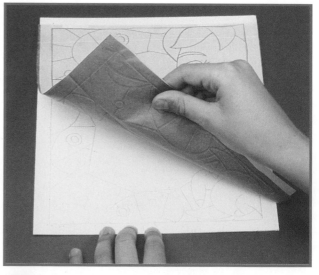

4 Remove the tracing paper, and the transfer paper, to reveal the design.

Pattern for the Fruity Flower Pot featured on pages 256–257.

Pattern for the Bumble Bee Spoon featured on pages 244–245.

Pattern for the Sun Wall Hanging featured on pages 248–249.

Pattern for the Monster Egg
featured on pages 258–259.

Pattern for the
Padlocked Money Box
featured on pages
252–253.

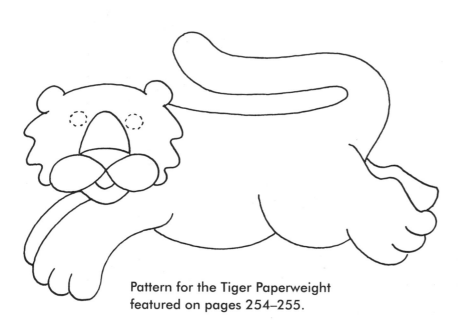

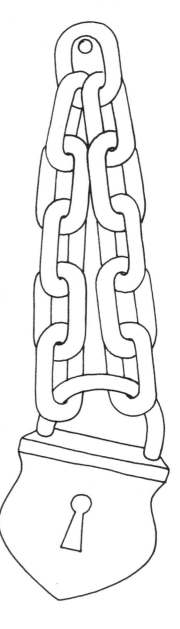

Pattern for the Tiger Paperweight
featured on pages 254–255.

Pattern for the Picasso Mirror featured on pages 260–261.

Papermaking
by David Watson

Papermaking is one of the oldest crafts. It was accidentally discovered in China around 105 AD by Ts'ai Lun, an imperial court official. He noticed that some old rags that had been left out in the rain had been broken down by the continuous pounding of passers-by, and had eventually dried to a hard flat sheet in the sun. Old fishing nets, ropes and rags were later used to make paper.

At first, paper was made for official documents and religious propaganda by the Chinese, Japanese and the nations of Islam. It eventually reached Europe around the twelfth century AD. The invention of the printing press in the early fifteenth century increased the demand for paper almost overnight. In Europe, the favoured material for papermaking was old rags that were bleached white. This tended to standardise the look of hand-made paper and make it appear rather bland. Some papermakers in places like Japan and Nepal continued to use a variety of plant fibres and as a result their hand-made paper looked much more beautiful.

When I was about ten years old I was given a sheet of European hand-made paper by my art teacher. It was yellowy white, quite stiff, with funny wavy edges. The texture looked something similar to that of an old blanket and it had a funny smell. I really wanted to cut off those edges and make it look neat. I was told that it was very special and very expensive. I felt so frightened of this piece of paper that I stuck it in a drawer, unable to use it for years and years. It is probably still there now.

Much later, somebody introduced me to a papermaker called Maureen Richardson and showed me some of her papers. 'That's not paper,' I said, 'it looks exciting, colourful and almost good enough to eat.' But it was paper. Maureen showed me how to make it and I was hooked. I could not believe the difference between that and the old stuffy, smelly and frightening piece of hand-made paper I had seen when I was younger.

This section contains lots of exciting techniques and projects. The materials always come from recycled or reclaimed sources where possible, and most of the equipment can be found at home. This section is about breaking the rules and having fun, so let's get started!

A **mould** and **deckle** are items made specially for papermaking. The mould is a frame covered with a mesh screen, and the deckle is a simple frame, the same size as the mould. Both these things can be bought from craft shops.

Techniques

The projects all follow the basic techniques shown here, with only slight variations. These techniques are based on traditional methods that are still used in hand-made paper mills today. Practise them until you are happy with your results, then you can start being really creative.

Note Exact paper quantities are not given. They will vary according to the type of paper that you are pulping. Generally, the more absorbent the paper is, the less you will need of it.

Making pulp

Paper can be broken down into tiny fibres by blending it into a pulp with water. The paper fibres are joined together again to form new sheets during the papermaking process. The colour of the paper you use for pulp will determine the colour of the new sheets.

 1 Prepare scrap paper for pulping by tearing it into 2.5cm (1in) squares.

 Food blenders have very sharp blades. Always ask an adult to help you use one.

2 Fill the food blender two-thirds full of water, then add a small handful of torn paper. Blend the mixture for approximately ten seconds.

Note Take care not to put too many pieces of paper in the food blender. You will know if you have because the sound will change if it is overloaded.

 3 Pour the blended pulp into a washing-up bowl half-full of clean water. Repeat these steps three more times.

Making a couching mound

A couching mound is a base on which you make your paper. You can make a couching mound out of a pile of wet newspapers.

1 Once you have prepared the pulp, you need to build up a couching mound. To do this, fold up five whole newspapers so that they are small enough to fit in a shallow plastic tray. Stack them in the tray, alternating the folds from one side of the pile to the other.

2 Fill the tray with water so that the newspapers are completely covered. Leave them to soak until they are all thoroughly wet, then drain off the excess water.

3 The couching mound should have a smooth surface that is slightly higher in the middle than at the edges. Press and rock the mesh screen on the mould across the top to make this shape.

4 Place a clean kitchen cloth over the couching mound to cover it.

From pulp to paper

This demonstration shows how to make one sheet of paper, but you can repeat the technique to make lots of sheets.

1 Once you have prepared the pulp and the couching mound you are ready to make your paper. Begin by stirring the pulp mixture vigorously with your hands.

2 Use a sponge to thoroughly wet the mesh screen on the mould. Then, hold the mould with the screen uppermost and place the deckle on top.

3 Insert the deckle and mould into the pulp mixture, right at the back of the bowl. Take them down to the bottom, and level them out.

Note Steps 3 and 4 should be one steady, continuous movement.

4 Pull the deckle and mould out of the mixture, making sure they stay level at all times.

 5

Carefully lift the deckle off the mould. Make sure that water does not drip on to the fibres, or your paper could be damaged.

 6

Turn the mould over then carefully position the front edge of the mould along the front edge of the couching mound.

Note Steps 7 and 8 should be one continuous movement.

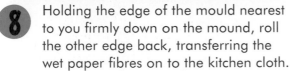

7 Roll the mould down on to the couching mound then press the far edge of it firmly into the mound.

8 Holding the edge of the mould nearest to you firmly down on the mound, roll the other edge back, transferring the wet paper fibres on to the kitchen cloth.

 9

Place a clean kitchen cloth over the fibres, making sure that it is completely flat, with no creases. Your first sheet of paper is now complete. Place another kitchen cloth on top, ready to make the next sheet of paper (see step 4, page 269).

Pressing and drying the paper

You may find it best to work outside when pressing paper. A lot of water will be squeezed out when you stand on the boards, and it can be quite messy!

Place a wooden board on the floor and lay two whole dry newspapers on top. Carefully transfer your newly-formed sheet(s) of paper with kitchen cloths from the couching mound on to the dry newspapers.

Place more dry newspapers and another board on top, then carefully stand on the boards, increasing the pressure slowly. Add more weight by asking your friend or an adult to help!

Remove the top board and the newspapers, then separate each set of two kitchen cloths, keeping a sheet of newly-formed paper in between. As this photograph shows, you do not have to worry about bending the sheets – by now the fibres will have joined together to form flexible sheets of paper.

Leave the sheets of paper to dry within the kitchen cloths on flat dry newspapers. Alternatively, you could hang them out to dry on a washing line.

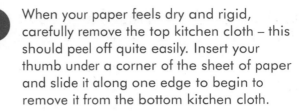

When your paper feels dry and rigid, carefully remove the top kitchen cloth – this should peel off quite easily. Insert your thumb under a corner of the sheet of paper and slide it along one edge to begin to remove it from the bottom kitchen cloth.

Repeat step 5 on an adjacent edge. Hold the free corner of the paper in one hand and carefully peel the paper away from the kitchen cloth.

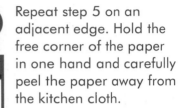

Sparkly Birthday Card

Cards became popular during the Victorian period when the first festive Christmas cards were produced. You can now buy a card for almost any occasion. This birthday card is made using the techniques shown on pages 268–273, but small sparkly shapes and a person's age are added. The shapes bond together in the dried sheet and the image is fixed on to the paper as it is being made.

YOU WILL NEED

White paper • Food blender
Washing-up bowl • Plastic tray
Newspaper • Jug • Mould and deckle
Sponge • 2 wooden boards
2 kitchen cloths • Glitter confetti
Thin coloured paper
Tea strainer • Pizza cutter
Ruler

1 Prepare some white paper pulp and a couching mound (see pages 268–269). Insert the deckle and mould into the pulp (see page 270), but rather than lifting them right out, bring them up level with the surface of the pulp and stop. Ask a friend to sprinkle glitter confetti over the deckle.

2 Separate the pieces of confetti if necessary, then slowly lift the deckle and mould out of the pulp and allow the water to drain out.

3 Carefully remove the deckle from the mould and turn the wet paper fibres out on to a couching mound. Tear some numbers out of thin coloured paper, then place them on one half of the wet paper fibres.

274

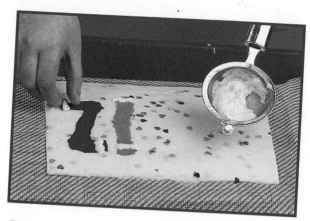

4 Use a tea strainer to remove some paper fibres from the pulp in the bowl. While the fibres are still very wet, place a thin line of them across each end of the numbers.

5 Cover with another kitchen cloth, then press and dry the paper (see pages 272–273). Use a ruler to mark the middle of the sheet then go over that line with a pizza cutter. Fold the paper in half to complete your card.

FURTHER IDEAS

Experiment with using seeds or leaves instead of glitter confetti – in fact, you can mix almost anything you like with the paper fibres.

Fancy Folder

YOU WILL NEED

Cartridge paper
Thick copper wire • Pliers
Food blender • Washing-up bowl
Plastic tray • Newspaper • Jug
Mould and deckle • Sponge
Ribbons • Old thick blanket
2 wooden boards
Pizza cutter • Ruler

Wonderful historical examples of patterned and textured paper can be seen in museums today. It is easy to recreate these effects using modern materials. Wire is used to make the design on this folder – it is bent into a design and placed under the wet paper fibres. Ribbons are placed between two layers of paper fibres. When the paper is dry, the wire is removed.

Bend a length of copper wire into a shape of your choice using a pair of pliers. The wire shape needs to be small enough to fit on to half of your sheet of paper.

Prepare some pulp made from cartridge paper, and a couching mound (see pages 268–269). Place a piece of old thick blanket on top of the mound.

Place the wire carefully on to the blanket so that the pattern will appear on one half of the paper.

Take up a layer of fibres in the mould and deckle, then turn them out over the wire. Peel back the mould carefully (see pages 270–271).

5 Wet the ribbons then place them over the fibres, a little way in from the top and bottom edges of the paper.

6 Take up another layer of paper fibres then carefully turn them out on top of the first layer. Remove the mould, cover with another piece of blanket, then press and dry the paper (see pages 272–273).

7 Remove the wire. Crease the middle of the sheet with a pizza cutter (see page 275) and fold it in half so that the raised pattern is on the front of the folder.

FURTHER IDEAS
Create your own patterns using different shapes — leaves, string or wire mesh. You can use anything that will make a mark.

Personal Paper

Watermarked papers became popular in Europe during the fifteenth century. You can only see a watermark when the paper is held up to the light. The marks made were usually of animals and fruits or simple shapes like the 'C' shown here. Why not make personalised paper with your own initials?

YOU WILL NEED

Cartridge paper
Thick and thin copper wire
Pliers to cut and bend the wire
Food blender • Washing-up bowl
Plastic tray • Newspaper
Jug • 2 kitchen cloths
Mould and deckle • Sponge
2 wooden boards

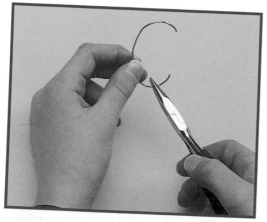

1 Use pliers to bend a length of thick copper wire into a 'C' shape. Make sure it will lie flat on a level surface.

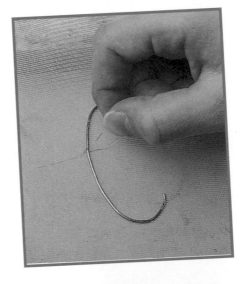

2 Place the 'C' on the mould's mesh surface. Fold short lengths of thin copper wire in half then poke the ends down through the mesh, either side of the 'C'.

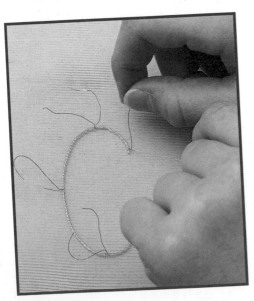

3 Hold the 'C' in place then turn the mould over. Twist the ends of the fine wire together so that the 'C' is held securely in place.

4 Make a very fine cartridge paper pulp by blending it slightly longer than usual (see page 268).

5 Make a couching mound and cover it with a kitchen cloth. Take up a layer of paper fibres in the mould and deckle, keeping them very level as you remove them from the pulp (see page 270).

Note If you can still see the wire 'C', the pulp is probably too thin, so make the pulp slightly thicker and try again.

6 Turn the paper fibres out on to the couching mound (see page 271). You should just be able to see the shape of the 'C' and there should be no bubbles or creases. Carefully cover the paper fibres with another kitchen cloth then press and dry the paper (see pages 272–273).

7 Hold your paper up to the light to see the watermark.

FURTHER IDEAS
Bend the wire into different shaped letters (you could make your own name) or use it to create simple patterns.

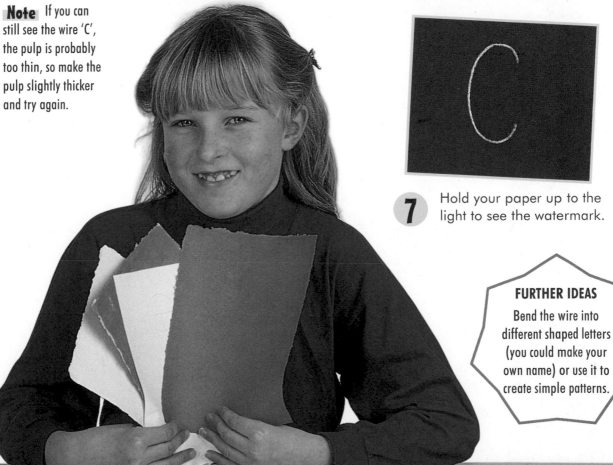

Feather Bookmarks

You can recycle all sorts of things and add them to the paper fibres – leaves, pieces of fabric, ribbons and more. Feathers are usually long and thin, so they make excellent bookmarks. This project allows you to make two bookmarks at once. You will need to prepare two bowls of pulp – one made from old printed paper and one from cartridge paper.

YOU WILL NEED

Thin foamboard • Old printed paper
White cartridge paper
Food blender • Washing-up bowl
Plastic tray • Newspaper • Jug
Mould and deckle • Cotton sheeting
Sponge • 2 flat feathers
Water-based matt varnish
2 wooden boards

1 Divide the deckle in half lengthways with a strip of foamboard.

2 Prepare the two bowls of pulp and make a couching mound (see pages 268–269). Cover the mound with cotton sheeting. Dip the mould and deckle in the printed paper pulp, lift it out and let the excess water drain off.

3 Remove the deckle then turn out the layer of wet paper fibres on to the cotton sheeting.

4 Thoroughly soak the feathers in clean water, then place one on each half of the wet paper fibres.

5 Make another layer of pulp with the cartridge paper then turn the paper fibres out over the feathers. Cover this layer of fibres with cotton sheeting, then press and dry the paper (see pages 272–273).

6 Apply a layer of varnish to the white side of the dry bookmarks, and watch the feathers magically appear.

FURTHER IDEAS

Add other things to the paper fibres instead of feathers. Try using sequins, pressed dried flowers or sparkling metallic threads.

Magic Picture Frame

Family photographs are often framed and displayed by proud relatives, or they are collected in treasured albums. If you have a favourite photograph you can show it off in this vibrant frame. Get an adult to help you colour-photocopy the photograph before you begin, making sure it is slightly smaller than the mesh on the mould. Two colours are used for this frame, and it combines magically with the photograph without you having to use any glue.

YOU WILL NEED
Coloured paper
Food blender • Washing-up bowl
Plastic tray • Newspaper
Cotton sheeting • Jug
Mould and deckle • Sponge
Plastic parcel tape • Coloured acetate
Photocopy of a photograph
2 wooden boards

Prepare one colour of pulp and a couching mound (see pages 268–269), then place a piece of cotton sheeting over the mound. Scoop up a layer of paper fibres and turn it out on to the cotton sheeting (see pages 270–271).

Place the photocopy of your photograph on top of the wet paper fibres.

Thoroughly dry the mesh screen on the mould, then stick strips of plastic parcel tape round the edge.

Cut a piece of acetate slightly smaller than the photocopied photograph, then place it on top of the mesh and hold it there with your thumbs. Prepare a second colour of pulp then dip the mould (without the deckle) into the pulp. Level it out under the surface, then carefully lift it out. The pulp will settle around the edges of the acetate.

Carefully peel the acetate away from the paper fibres to leave a border.

Turn the border out over the picture. Cover with another piece of cotton sheeting then press and dry the paper in the usual way (see pages 272–273).

FURTHER IDEAS
Choose different colours for your border, and add glitter confetti or pressed dried flowers to the paper fibres.

String-Along Book

You can recycle old paper to make this beautiful book, which can have as many pages as you like. The paper has a great texture and is perfect for chalk or pastel drawings, or you can simply write on it with a pen. You can make front and back covers for the book using thicker paper if you wish.

 Prepare some pulp and a couching mound (see pages 268–269), then place a piece of old thick blanket on top of the mound. Turn out a layer of paper fibres on top (see pages 270–271). Thoroughly wet the string then cut it in half. Arrange one end of each length of string on the paper fibres as shown.

 Turn out a second layer of paper fibres over the string to complete the first page of the book, then place two pieces of blanket on top.

3 Make the first layer of paper fibres for the second page of the book. Take the string across the couching mound, leaving short loops on one side. Make the second layer of paper fibres then turn this out over the string.

Note This stage can be a bit tricky, so do not hurry it.

4 Continue making more pages, moving the string from one side to the other, until you have made about ten pages. Lift the wet paper fibres and blanket layers on to a wooden board. Put another board on top and press out all the water (see page 272).

5 Place the pressed pile at one end of your work surface. Ask a friend to hold the bottom page down, then carefully open out the linked pages. Put dry newspapers below and on top of each page to soak up the moisture. Remove the pieces of blanket when all the pages are dry.

FURTHER IDEAS
Make the book into a large wall hanging by linking more sheets at the top and bottom as well as at the sides.

Funny Face Lampshade

This project shows you how easy it is to make your own lampshade. The pulp you will use is made from tracing paper. This has very short fibres, and all kinds of strange things happen as they dry. In fact, it is just about impossible to keep them flat!

Electricity and water can be very dangerous together. Ask an adult to disconnect the table lamp from the electricity supply before you start this project.

YOU WILL NEED

Low-energy light bulb, maximum 15 watt
Table lamp base • Tracing paper
1m (3$\frac{1}{2}$ft) of stiff copper wire
Pliers • Sticky tape • Food blender
Washing-up bowl • Plastic tray
Newspaper • Jug • Mould and deckle
Sponge • Old thick blanket
2 wooden boards

 Take the copper wire and place the centre of it against the lamp fitting. Carefully wrap it once around the base of the fitting.

 Loosen the wire carefully from around the base of the lamp fitting and remove it, taking care not to alter the shape. Use the pliers to bend the rest of the wire into an interesting face shape. Make sure the neck is at least 7.5cm (3in) long.

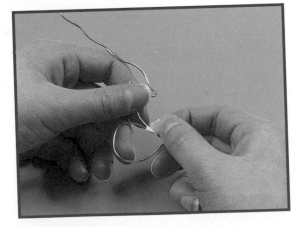

 Join the two ends together with sticky tape.

5
Place the wire shape over the first layer of paper fibres, leaving the neck end free.

4
Prepare some tracing paper pulp and a couching mound (see pages 268–269), then place a piece of old thick blanket on top of the mound. Turn out a layer of paper fibres on to the blanket (see pages 270–271).

Note The tracing paper pulp should be finely blended for this project.

6
Turn out another layer of paper fibres over the wire shape. Carefully place a second piece of blanket on top, then press and dry thoroughly (see pages 272–273). Ease the wire back over the lamp fitting then bend the paper up in front of the light bulb.

FURTHER IDEAS
Try making different wire shapes such as stars and moons, and add glitter to the paper fibres so that the lamp shade sparkles in the light.

Pulp Painting

You can create amazing paintings using pulp made from recycled coloured paper – swirls and circles of bright colour can be combined or blended to make abstract or realistic designs. The colours will lighten when they dry, so use really brightly coloured paper to make your pulp. In this project, the pulp is not diluted in a washing-up bowl. Instead, it is poured straight into the mould and deckle which sits in a shallow tray of water.

YOU WILL NEED

Coloured paper
Food blender • 3 plastic cups
2 plastic trays • Newspaper
Jug • Mould and deckle
2 kitchen cloths • Sponge
2 wooden boards
Paintbrush

 Prepare three different colours of pulp (see page 268) then pour each colour into a cup. Make a couching mound (see page 269).

2 Place the mould and deckle into a shallow tray. Fill the tray with water until it is almost level with the top of the deckle.

3 Hold the deckle down to stop it floating off the mould, then pour one colour of pulp into the deckle, starting at one edge.

4 Add another colour of pulp, leaving a space between the two colours. Add the third colour in the same way.

5 Use the end of a paintbrush to blend the colours together so that there are no gaps or holes. Add more pulp if necessary.

6 When you are happy with your picture, carefully lift the mould and deckle out of the water. Allow the excess water to drain away, then continue making the paper as shown on page 271. Press and dry the paper (see pages 272–273).

FURTHER IDEAS
Make more colours of pulp and use them to paint a simple landscape.

Patterned Paper

In this project you can recycle your paper to create vibrantly coloured patterns. A gravy baster or an empty squeezy bottle can be filled with coloured pulp and used to squirt out designs and shapes. The pulp has to be blended finely so it does not clog up the nozzle of the gravy baster. It will be just right when it looks and feels like soft ice-cream.

YOU WILL NEED

Coloured paper
Food blender
Plastic tray • 4 plastic cups
Gravy baster
Mould and deckle
Kitchen cloth

1 Make up four colours of pulp (see page 268) then pour each colour into a cup.

2 Place the mould in the tray and thoroughly wet the mesh with a kitchen cloth. Position the deckle on top of the mould.

3 Squeeze the end of the gravy baster then dip the nozzle into one of the colours of pulp. Gently release your hold to draw up the pulp.

4 Move the gravy baster over the mesh then gently squeeze the end so that the paper fibres flow from the nozzle on to the mesh. Continue until you have covered it completely.

5 Clean the gravy baster with water. Change to a second colour of pulp and start painting your pattern.

6 Continue adding the colours until you are happy with your pattern.

FURTHER IDEAS
Make a simple picture using this technique — try a boat on a stormy sea, a dinosaur or a fantasy landscape.

7 Leave the paper to dry naturally on the mould, then carefully peel it away from the mesh.

Paperfolding

by Clive Stevens

Paperfolding is not only an ancient art, but it is one that requires very little equipment or space. As long as you have paper, a pair of scissors and some glue you can create a variety of wonderful sculptural shapes.

The art of paperfolding is thought to date back to the first or second century AD in China. The Japanese were practising this art by the sixth century and they called it origami (pronounced or-i-GA-me). The word is made up from 'ori', the Japanese word for folding, and 'kami', the word for paper.

In Japan, paper was scarce long ago, so only wealthy people could afford to do paperfolding. But as easier methods of papermaking were developed, paper became less expensive and paperfolding became a popular art for everyone.

The Japanese were not the only people folding paper. The Moors from North Africa were also practising this art. Their religion forbade the creation of representational figures, so their paperfolding took the form of geometric decorative designs, and they took their techniques with them when they invaded Spain during the eighth century. From there, paperfolding spread to South America, then to other parts of Europe as trade routes opened up, and later it spread to the United States. In Victorian England, it became a popular children's pastime. Paper hats, similar to the square hat worn by the carpenter in Lewis Carroll's *Alice Through the Looking Glass*, were made.

In this section you begin with basic scoring and folding techniques, then go on to enjoy making a pirate hat, a glider plane, an animal mask and many other exciting projects. You can also have fun designing and creating your own ideas. Be inventive by using different textured paper like thin corrugated card, brown wrapping paper, metallic and handmade paper. Or try using patterned paper such as gift wrap, wallpaper or pages from a magazine.

With paperfolding you can create wonderful greetings cards for your friends and family and design interesting gift wrap for a special present. So, have fun – and happy paperfolding!

Techniques

There are several basic paperfolding techniques. Freehand folding is simply folding paper without scoring or measuring the paper or card. To create intricate shapes it is helpful to score the paper or card first with a blunt instrument. Folding away from you makes a valley fold. Folding towards you makes a mountain fold. These are shown in the patterns as dots and dashes for valley folds, and dashes for mountain folds (see page 314).

Scoring straight lines

Place a ruler on the piece of card, where you want the line to be. Use the ruler as a guide and run an empty ballpoint pen along the edge to make an indent in the paper.

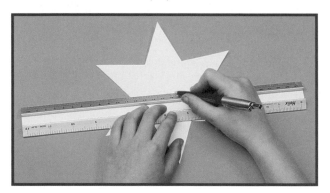

Hard-folding

Fold the card over along the line you have scored. To hard-fold, use the side of your fingernail to make a neat fold along the scored line.

Scoring curves

Cut out a cardboard template of the shape you need. Run an empty ballpoint pen along the edge of the template to make an indent in the paper. Alternatively, you can score a curve freehand.

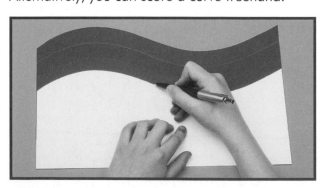

Soft-folding

Gently pinch along the scored line with your fingers. Repeat several times.

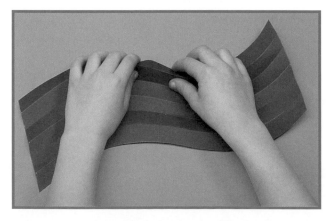

Making a template

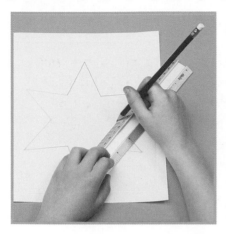

 1
Place a piece of tracing paper over the pattern (see pages 314–317). Tape it down with small pieces of masking tape. Trace around the outline using a pencil. You can use a ruler if the pattern has straight lines. Remove the tape from the tracing paper.

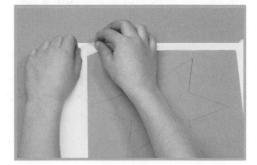

2
Place a piece of carbon paper face down on the surface you want to transfer the design on to. Place the tracing over the top then tape it in place.

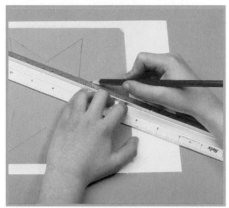

3
Trace around the outline with a pencil. Again, use a ruler for any straight lines.

4
Remove the tracing paper and carbon paper to reveal the transferred image.

Pirate Hat

This project only requires simple freehand folding and it is an age-old favourite. It was popular with Victorian children when they played at being pirates. The hat can be embellished by attaching cut-out designs, such as a skull and crossbones, or you could attach a feather if you want to make a Robin Hood hat.

1 Take a piece of black paper, the same size as an unfolded tabloid newspaper, and hard-fold it in half lengthways (see page 294).

2 Hard-fold the paper in half lengthways again.

3 Open up the last fold, then fold down the left-hand corner to the centre line. Repeat with the other corner.

4 Fold up the bottom edge nearest to you so that it meets the corners. Fold it up the same amount again. Turn the hat over and repeat on the other side.

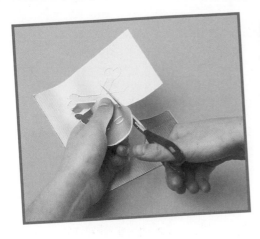

5

Trace the skull and crossbones pattern shown on page 317 on to metallic card (see page 295). Use scissors to cut out the main shape, and a craft knife to cut out the small shapes inside.

Craft knives are very sharp. Ask an adult to cut out the small shapes.

6

Fold the skull and crossbones in half lengthways, then glue it to the front of the hat, making sure that it lies over the central fold.

FURTHER IDEAS

Make a Robin Hood hat using different coloured paper. Using scissors, cut out a feather shape from card, score it down the middle then cut lots of slits in it.

Glider Plane

Your mother or father may have folded wonderful paper aeroplanes for you when you were younger. Well, here is one that you can easily make yourself, using freehand folding, soft-folding and one piece of coloured paper. The plane is decorated with cut-out thin coloured paper shapes which are glued on to the wings. You should never launch your finished plane towards other people.

YOU WILL NEED
Coloured paper
Scissors • PVA glue
Paper clip

 Cut a piece of coloured paper approximately 25cm x 28cm (8½in x 11in). Score and soft-fold it in half lengthways (see page 294), then fold the top corners down to the centre line.

 Fold each side in from the point, to meet the centre line.

 Fold the tip back towards the middle, to the point where the sides meet to form the front of the plane.

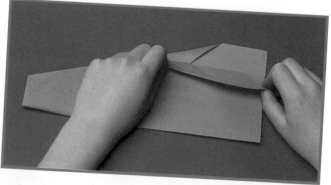

 Fold the plane in half lengthways, then fold the top wing down about 1cm (½in). Turn the plane over and repeat on the other wing.

298

5 Fold the wing down again, from the top of the nose. Turn the plane over and repeat on the other wing.

6 Flatten the plane out. Cut out your own decoration from coloured paper, then glue the shapes on to the wings.

7 Fold the plane ready for flight, add a paper clip to the nose and you are ready for take-off!

FURTHER IDEAS
Make a whole squadron of planes and hang them from your bedroom ceiling, or from a coat hanger, to make a mobile.

Spinning Windmill

This simple design is made from brightly coloured thin card and decorated with different size dots in a contrasting colour. When the windmill spins, it forms wonderful coloured patterns. The handle is made by scoring lines along a length of thin card which is folded into a triangular stick.

YOU WILL NEED
Coloured paper
Thin card • Empty ballpoint pen
Ruler • Pencil • Scissors
PVA glue • Craft knife
Cutting mat
Brass split pin

1 Cut out a piece of coloured paper approximately 20cm (8in) square. Cut out some shapes from a different coloured paper and glue them on to the square.

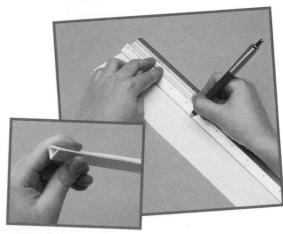

2 Use a ruler and pencil to draw two diagonal lines through the square to form a cross. Make a cut at each corner, exactly one third of the way along the pencil line.

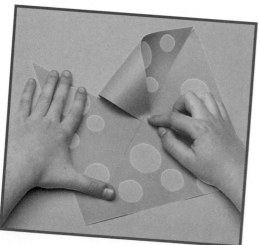

3 Pull one of the points down just past the centre and glue it in place. Hold it for a few moments until it is dry. Repeat with the other three points.

4 Cut out a rectangle of thin card, 4cm x 30cm (2in x 11¾in). Mark and score three lines 1cm (½in) apart. Fold along the lines, then form the card into a triangular stick. Glue in place and hold until dry.

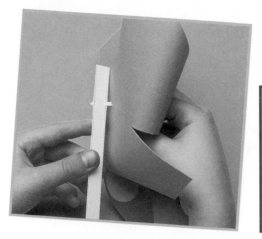

5 Use a craft knife to cut a very small slit in one end of the stick approximately 2cm (¾in) from the end. Make sure that it goes all the way through to the other side. Using scissors, cut a small hole in the centre of the windmill; push a split pin through it, then through the paper stick.

6 Carefully fold back the ends of the split pin, so that the windmill can turn.

FURTHER IDEAS

Make some colourful miniature windmills, tape them to cocktail sticks, then display them in a small vase or container.

Twisted Pot

With simple folds you can create some colourful crazy containers – and this ingenious little twisted pot is a wonderful example of cardboard engineering. You can decorate it with paper shapes, then fold and glue it to form a square box shape. With a simple twist it suddenly springs to life.

YOU WILL NEED
Thin coloured card
Coloured paper
Tracing paper • Carbon paper
Masking tape • Pencil
Empty ballpoint pen
Scissors • Ruler
PVA glue

1 Transfer the design shown on page 316 on to thin coloured card (see page 295). Cut out the rectangular shape. Score the card along the vertical and diagonal lines using an empty ballpoint pen and a ruler (see page 294).

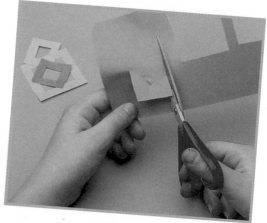

2 Cut out shapes of your choice from coloured paper.

3 Use PVA glue to stick the paper shapes to the card. Leave to dry.

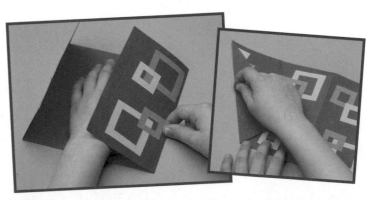

4 Hard-fold along all of the scored lines (see page 294). Turn the card pattern face-down and fold the vertical lines towards you. Turn the card over then fold the diagonal lines towards you.

5 Glue the flap to the other end to form an open-ended box. Hold between your finger and thumb for a few moments, then leave to dry thoroughly.

6 Flatten the box. Slowly push your thumbs together, then very gently twist your right hand towards you so that the pot springs into shape.

FURTHER IDEAS
You could make a set of small brightly coloured pots which can be used as egg cups for the whole family.

Bat Mobile

This fun mobile uses black and contrasting metallic card, so that when the stars and moon turn they reflect the light beautifully. The shapes are traced from the patterns, cut out and scored to create a three dimensional image. They are then suspended by thread on a coat hanger, but you could use an ordinary wooden stick or a wire rod.

YOU WILL NEED

Black and thin metallic card
Tracing paper • Carbon paper
Masking tape • Pencil
Scissors • Empty ballpoint pen
Ruler • Sharp pencil
Cotton thread • Clear sticky tape
Coat hanger

1 Transfer the bat, moon and star patterns from page 315 on to black and thin metallic card (see page 295). Cut out the shapes.

2 Score and then hard-fold the stars (see page 294) then open them up to form three-dimensional forms.

3 Score along the curved centre line of each moon and then soft-fold gently (see page 294).

4 Score each bat freehand, then soft-fold to give shape to the body and wings.

5 Thread lengths of cotton through the holes and secure on the underside with clear sticky tape.

Ask an adult to help you suspend your mobile from a suitable location.

Note You can adjust the way your mobile hangs by adding small pieces of removable adhesive to the pieces.

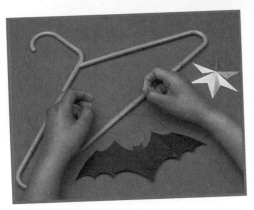

 6 Tie the cotton on to a coat hanger to suspend the moon, stars and bats at different levels. Snip off any loose ends.

FURTHER IDEAS

You could cover the coat hanger with crepe paper. Decorate it with cut-out cloud shapes or shiny stars.

Pleated Picture Frame

Every artist needs a beautiful frame for a favourite picture or painting. It completes the effect and complements the image it surrounds. This project shows you how to create a simple pleated frame. The sides are glued on to a corrugated cardboard base and pleated corners are added in a contrasting colour.

YOU WILL NEED

Single corrugated cardboard
Thin coloured card
Scissors • Ruler
Empty ballpoint pen
Tracing paper • Carbon paper
Masking tape • Pencil
PVA glue

 Cut out a piece of corrugated cardboard 22cm x 25cm (8¾in x 10in). Draw a line 5cm (2in) in from each edge with a ruler and pencil. Cut out the centre to form a frame.

2 Cut out 2 strips of thin coloured card 6cm x 30cm (2¼in x 11¾in) and 2 strips 6cm x 27cm (2¼in x 10¾in).

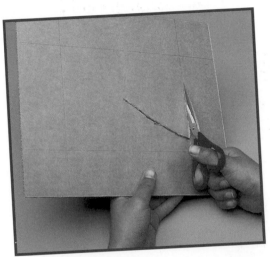

3 Mark lines 1.5cm (⅝in) apart all along each strip of coloured card. Pleat each strip by scoring and then hard-folding along the lines (see page 294).

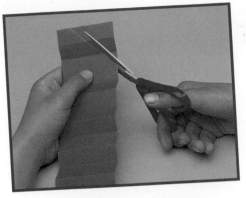

Open the pleated strips out. Mark a diagonal line from the third fold approximately 1cm (½in) in from the corner. Cut the corner off. Repeat on all ends of the coloured card strips.

Apply glue to the cardboard base, then position the pleated strips on top. Leave to dry.

Transfer the pattern on page 315 on to coloured card four times (see page 295). Cut them out, score and pleat them, then glue them on to each corner to hide the joins.

FURTHER IDEAS
You can use circles or other shapes on the corners, and experiment with different sized pleats to create different effects.

Bird and Worm Card

It is always nice to receive and send homemade cards. This pop-up card will amuse your family and friends and it can be used for any occasion. It uses a simple fold to create the pop-up action. The bird's head is transferred from the pattern and glued to the card. A slit is then cut along the beak and folded back. For the finishing touch a pink worm is added to the inside of the beak.

YOU WILL NEED

Coloured paper
Thin card • Scissors
Tracing paper • Carbon paper
Masking tape • Pencil
PVA Glue

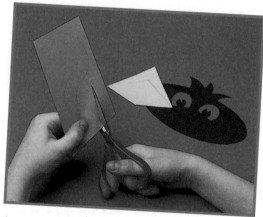

1 Transfer the bird and worm patterns on page 315 on to coloured paper (see page 295). Cut out the shapes.

2 Cut out a piece of thin card approximately 36cm x 26cm (14¼in x 10¼in). Fold the card in half, and then in half again.

3 Unfold the card once and lay it flat, with the first fold at the top. Glue the beak on to the bird, then glue the bird on to the inside of the open card.

4 Open the card up completely. Fold it inside out and cut a slit along the line on the beak.

5 Hard-fold the top of the beak up, and the bottom of the beak back (see page 294).

6 Re-fold the card and pull the beak up to open the mouth. Fold the worm over the bottom of the beak and glue it in place inside the mouth.

FURTHER IDEAS

You can adapt the patterns to make other animals. Try making a frog with a fly in its mouth. The worm can become the frog's tongue and you can use tracing paper to make the wings for the fly.

Treasure Chest

Everyone has a collection of different things that they treasure and want to keep safe or hidden away. It could be special pebbles, shiny beads or secret messages. This little treasure chest is just the thing to store them in. It is made to look like the real thing by using a black marker pen to add the bolt heads and a lock.

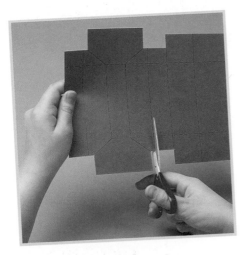

1 Transfer the basic chest pattern on page 314 on to thin coloured card (see page 295). Cut out the shape, then cut along the solid cut lines.

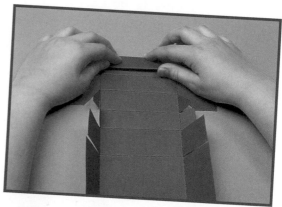

2 Score and hard-fold along all the dotted lines (see page 294).

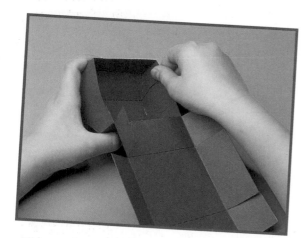

3 Glue the back of the angled tabs 1, 2, 3, 4 to the inside of the lid ends. Now glue tabs 5, 6, 7, 8 to the inside of the lid ends in the same way, to complete the lid.

4 Glue the back of the corner tabs 9, 10, 11 and 12 to the inside of the base ends to form a box.

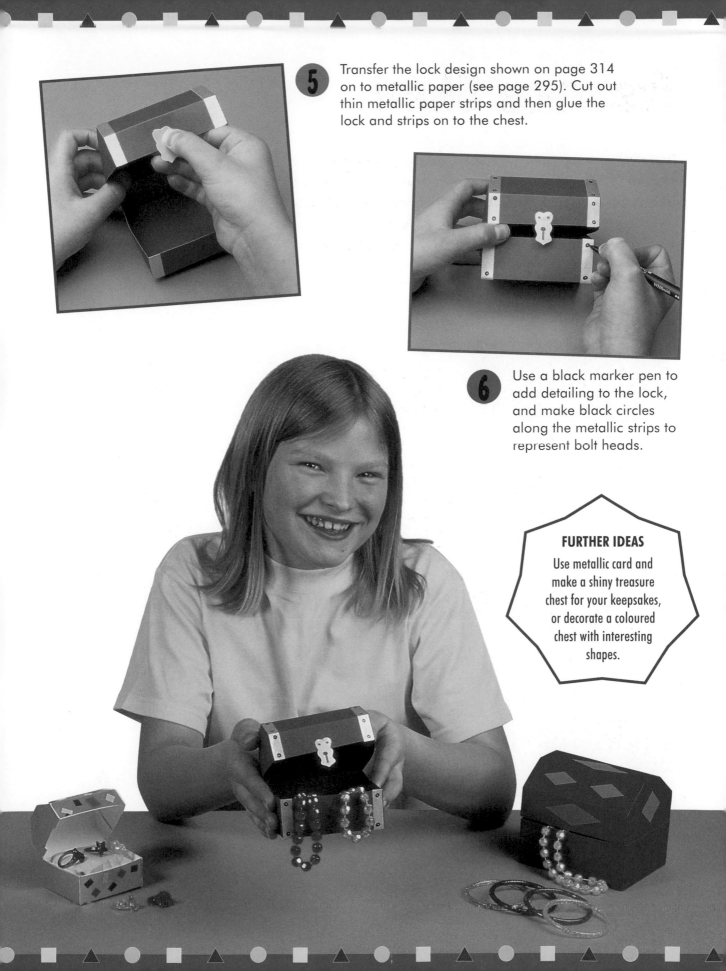

5 Transfer the lock design shown on page 314 on to metallic paper (see page 295). Cut out thin metallic paper strips and then glue the lock and strips on to the chest.

6 Use a black marker pen to add detailing to the lock, and make black circles along the metallic strips to represent bolt heads.

FURTHER IDEAS

Use metallic card and make a shiny treasure chest for your keepsakes, or decorate a coloured chest with interesting shapes.

Elephant Mask

Everyone loves masks. They are great fun to make and wear and they can transform you into something, or someone, completely different. This project is easy to do and it can be adapted if you want to create a different animal.

YOU WILL NEED
Thin black card
Thin coloured card • Tracing paper
Carbon paper • Masking tape
Pencil • Stapler
Empty ballpoint pen • Ruler
Scissors • Craft knife
Cutting mat

(!)

Ask an adult to help you when you staple. The flat side of the staple must be next to the head.

1 Cut out a piece of thin black card approximately 70cm x 50cm (27½in x 19¾in). Fold the card in half widthways, then align the marked edge of the basic mask pattern on page 316 along the fold. Transfer the pattern on to the card (see page 295), then cut out the shapes.

2 Open up the mask and fit the side tabs around your head. Hold them in position, remove the mask then staple the ends. Replace the mask on your head and take the front strip over the top of your head. Hold in position, remove and staple in place.

3 Transfer the face, ears and trunk patterns on pages 316 and 317 on to thin coloured card. Cut them out. Score along the fold lines of the trunk (see page 294) and then form it into pleats.

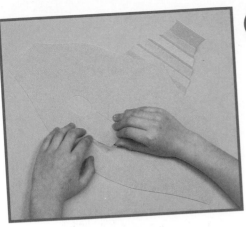

 Use scissors to cut out the eye holes. Use a craft knife to cut a slit in the face where the trunk goes. Insert the trunk into the slit and tape in place.

 Craft knives are sharp. Ask an adult to cut the slit in the trunk.

FURTHER IDEAS
You can adapt the pattern and use different coloured card to make a pig mask.

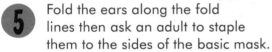 Fold the ears along the fold lines then ask an adult to staple them to the sides of the basic mask.

Ask an adult to attach the face to the basic mask with staples, making sure the eyes line up.

Patterns

Enlarge these patterns on a photocopier by 200%, then use them to make the templates for the projects (see page 295).

The patterns show two types of fold. Sometimes you need to fold the paper away from you. These folds are called valley folds. They are shown as dots and dashes. When you fold towards you, it's called a mountain fold. These folds are shown as dashes.

Get an adult to help you photocopy the patterns.

—·—·—·—·—·—·—· Valley fold – fold away from you

----------------------- Mountain fold – fold towards you

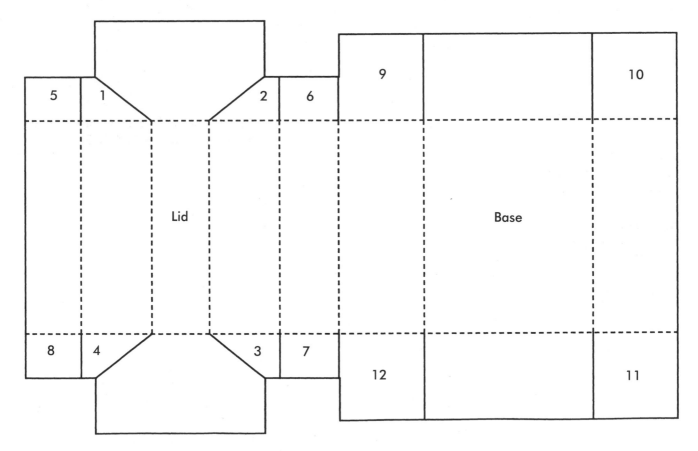

Patterns for the Treasure Chest featured on pages 310–311.

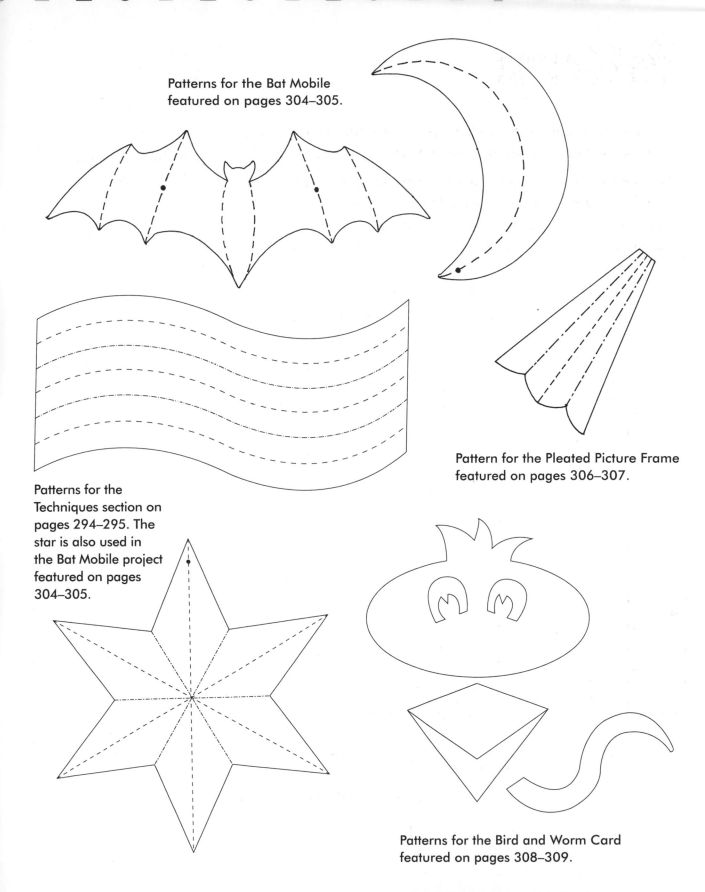

Patterns for the Bat Mobile featured on pages 304–305.

Patterns for the Techniques section on pages 294–295. The star is also used in the Bat Mobile project featured on pages 304–305.

Pattern for the Pleated Picture Frame featured on pages 306–307.

Patterns for the Bird and Worm Card featured on pages 308–309.

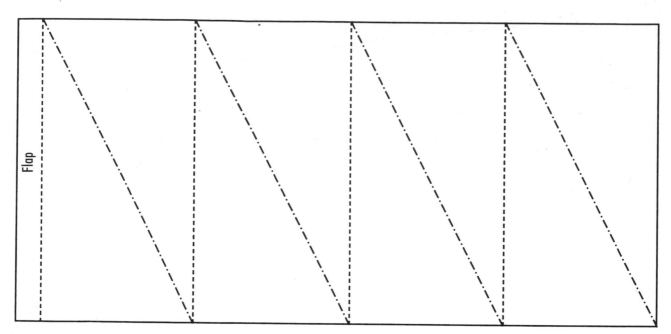

Flap

Pattern for the Twisted Pot
featured on pages 302–303.

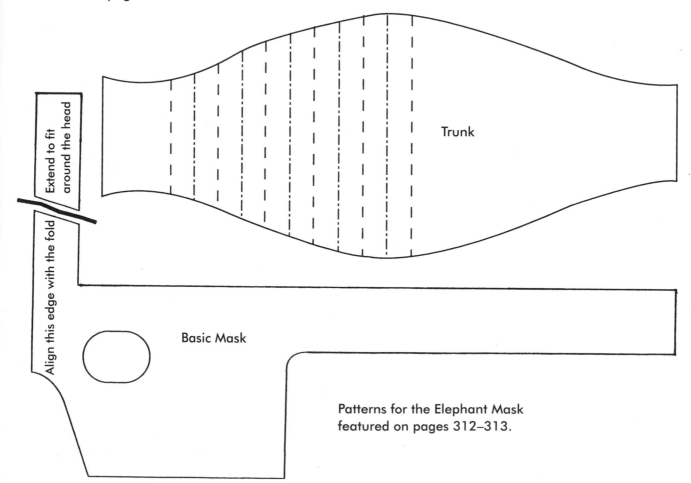

Trunk

Extend to fit
around the head

Align this edge with the fold

Basic Mask

Patterns for the Elephant Mask
featured on pages 312–313.

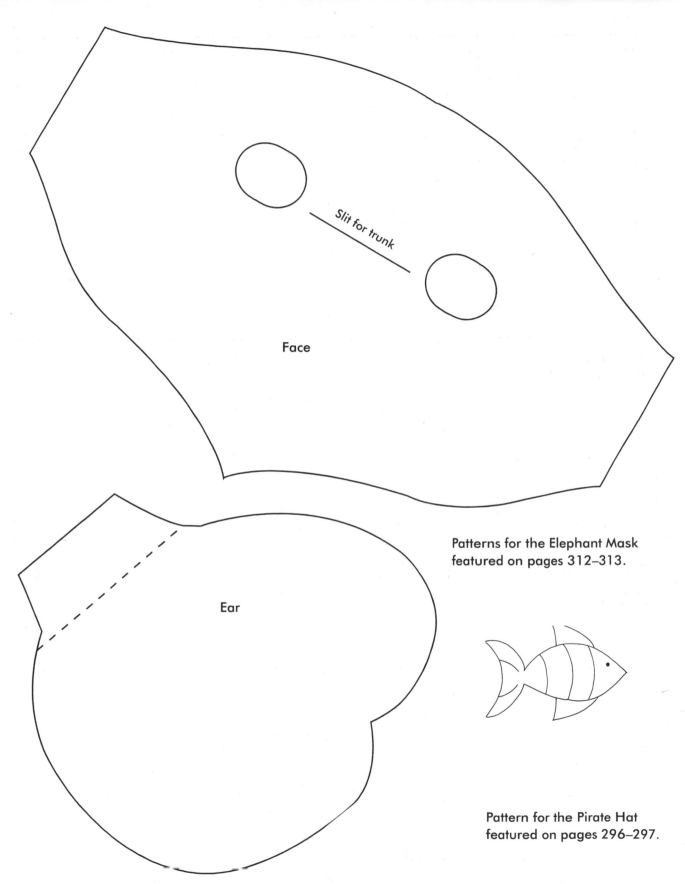

Slit for trunk

Face

Patterns for the Elephant Mask featured on pages 312–313.

Ear

Pattern for the Pirate Hat featured on pages 296–297.

About the authors

Judy Balchin studied art at Cardiff College of Art and then specialized in graphic design at Kent Institute of Art and Design. She now designs craft kits for both adults and children, and runs workshops for all ages. Judy has appeared on television as a craft demonstrator and her craft techniques have been featured in DVDs. She frequently writes articles for art and craft magazines.

Michelle Powell studied art and design at Bath College of Higher Education. She majored in paper making and graduated with a degree in teaching art. A crafter at heart, Michelle has a passion for paper, beads and fabric and has crafted as long as she can remember. She has worked as a craft product designer and magazine contributor, prior to becoming editor of **Scrapbook Magic** and **Practical Crafts**. Michelle is now a craft designer and author.

Tamsin Carter studied graphic design at Kingsway College, London. She was a book designer for a number of years and now runs a successful book, graphic and web design business, Pynto Ltd. She enjoys many crafts, most recently using beads, foam and wire as well as silver clay and jewellery making. She always makes the special people in her life handmade cards and really enjoys making each one different. She lives in Devon with her husband, Steve, two children and three cats.

Clive Stevens studied art and design in Canada, where he then worked as a graphic designer, art director and illustrator. He ran his own advertising agency in the UK for 20 years. Clive has written four books on paperfolding and paper sculpture. He has run weekend courses in paper sculpture and written articles on paperfolding techniques for **Crafts Magazine** and **The Artist**. He has also produced paper sculpture animations for television advertising. He presently creates paper sculptures for sale throughout the world, and travels around British schools demonstrating paper crafts.

Greta Speechley studied at Hornsey College of Art. She worked as a television graphic designer for many years on title sequences, commercials and special effects. Alongside this, she was tapestry weaving, painting, and making ceramics, selling through craft fairs and galleries. She has held many workshops for both children and adults. She is also the author of the ***Crafts for Kids*** series of books published in the USA. She teaches A-level Art Textiles and is developing her own storyboard for a children's animation film.

David Watson is an artist who specialises in experimental papermaking techniques and he is the author of ***Creative Handmade Paper***, published by Search Press. He carries out regular commissions and has exhibited his work throughout Britain and in the USA. David has been involved in a number of artist-in-residence schemes, many of which were at schools and colleges. He gives demonstrations of his work and conducts workshops for groups of all ages. He also teaches students to degree level. David lives in Brighton. He is an avid collector of discarded and recycled materials which he uses for public art commissions

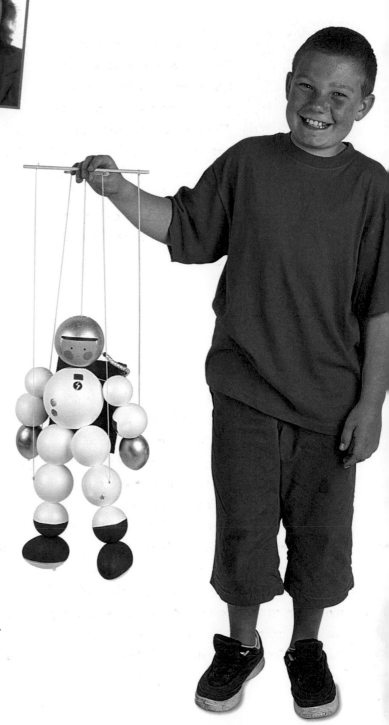